The UNIX Audit

Using UNIX to Audit UNIX

Other McGraw-Hill Titles of Interest

The UNIX Audit

Using UNIX to Audit UNIX

Michael G. Grottola

McGraw-Hill, Inc.

New York San Francisco Washington, D.C. Auckland Bogotá
Caracas Lisbon London Madrid Mexico City Milan
Montreal New Delhi San Juan Singapore
Sydney Tokyo Toronto

Library of Congress Cataloging-in-Publication Data

Grottola, Michael G.
    The UNIX audit: using UNIX to audit UNIX / by Michael G.
  Grottola.

        p.   cm.
    Includes index.
    ISBN 0-07-025127-4 (pbk.)
    1. Operating systems (Computers)   2. UNIX (Computer file)
  3. Electronic data processing—Auditing.   I. Title.
  QA76.76.O63G77   1993
  005.4'3—dc20   92-35733
                                                      CIP

        3 4 5 6 7 8 9 0   DOC/DOC   0 9 8 7 6 5 4 3

ISBN 0-07-025127-4

The editors for this book were Neil Levine and Marianne Krcma.
The production supervisor was Katherine G. Brown, and the
New York production supervisor was Suzanne Babeuf.
This book was set in ITC Century Light. It was composed
by TAB Books.

Printed and bound by R.R. Donnelley & Sons Company.

Aviion is a trademark of Data General Corporation.
CompuServe is a trademark of Compuserve, Inc.
IBM is a trademark of International Business Machines, Inc.
MS-DOS is a trademark of Microsoft Corporation.
UNIX is a trademark of AT&T.

For more information about other McGraw-Hill materials,
call 1-800-2-MCGRAW in the United States. In other
countries, call your nearest McGraw-Hill office.

 This book is printed on recycled, acid-free paper containing a minimum of 50% recycled de-
inked fiber.

There are a number of people who have helped and encouraged me to write this book: my wife, Kathleen, and our family; friends; and not the least of which all of Business Resources' past customers. Special thanks goes to Ken Anderson, President of View Point Technologies, who permitted me to use his company's Aviion workstation for several months during the creation of the shell scripts contained in appendix A.

Contents

Introduction

Webster defines *audit* as follows:

1. *A formal examination and verification of an account book. A methodical examination and review.*
2. *The final report of the books of examination by auditors.*
3. *To examine with intent to verify . . ..*

After a decade or so of discovery, introduction, and extensive use, UNIX has come a long way. It's being used in places and in ways never envisioned by its original authors.

This book is not intended to tell you how good UNIX is or convince you to use it for anything and everything. Nor does it teach you how to develop software using UNIX.

My intent is to help business managers, MIS directors, system administrators, and consultants find out "just what's going on here." This book is about gaining control of that powerful body of software, UNIX. Why bother, you might ask? During the years of the "UNIX guru," many came to believe that the rich set of utility software bundled with most UNIX systems, plus those created for any specific site's usage, were sufficient to justify the purchase and use of UNIX-based systems.

This approach is no longer productive. At first, discovery and exploration of UNIX was important. Focusing on it as a new set of tools was necessary. Like a child growing to maturity, that inward focus by the UNIX community must come to an end. There is ample evidence that the UNIX community itself believes the time has come to ensure that UNIX is more commercially viable. The current attention to standards and uniform user interfaces are examples of a community moving away from specialized and somewhat cryptic uses to mainstream usage.

This book is a contribution to the effort to bring UNIX to the mainstream user. It's time to turn attention to the productive use of these tools for those who fund such efforts: private and public enterprises. To do this, UNIX must be controllable by its owners. This book will put you in control and keep you there.

You will learn to take control of a UNIX system that might be somewhat foreign to you. Even though you are probably not a programmer or technician, properly auditing a UNIX system will enable you to control it. How do you measure UNIX? This book shows you, as auditor, what to look for in the system, how to examine it, and how to report your findings.

Chapter 1 sets up the issue of doing an audit in a broad sense. It discusses the larger context within which your audit will be done. It addresses things that should be done and understood before doing the audit.

Chapter 2 describes the outline and contents of the written documents that will contain the results of the audit. This is done early on in the book so that you have a clear idea of where the UNIX audit is going.

Chapter 3 sets forth certain prerequisites that are required to execute the UNIX audit. These involve both consulting skills and computer literacy skills. The chapter also includes a reference of UNIX commands that have particular audit value. (Don't worry; there is no need to completely master their use in order to perform the UNIX audit.)

Chapter 4 introduces concepts key to examining the static UNIX system: files, their contents, and their integrity. Baseline creation is the key to establishing an audit reference point. In this chapter, the UNIX audit baseline is defined and described in detail.

Chapter 5 shows you how to conduct interviews with the users of the system, as well as what documents to review and what to look for.

Chapter 6 describes how to conduct the file system examination using software tools supplied with this book.

Chapter 7 focuses on examining the dynamics of a UNIX system by describing how to conduct the system performance examination with tools native to UNIX.

Chapter 8 provides tips on how to present the audit results.

Chapter 9 concludes the body of the book with the presentation and discussion of useful forms to include in your audit report.

Five appendices found at the end of this book are referred to in the body of the book:

- Appendix A, program listings

- Appendix B, the contents of TLIST

- Appendix C, report samples (audit README, directory README, DIFFERENCE)

- Appendix D, a sample sizing estimator for a production database

- Appendix E, a graph illustrating an action plan and associated costs

1

Audit Basics

It's Monday morning. You arrive at your office to find your key technical staff has resigned en masse to start their own business. Before you go home sick, realize that there is a way to get control of that UNIX system you've been paying for, for years, but have successfully steered clear of until now.

Barring a malicious attempt to destroy your company's records, you can find out exactly what you have, and what you can do with a system that might have intimidated you. UNIX itself can be used to find out everything you need to know to understand and document the system that controls a part, or all, of your business.

Corporate computing facilities are expensive, critical resources. Their performance, like that of key employees and departments, should be evaluated on a regular basis for relevancy, effectiveness, and optimization. Waiting until the "Monday morning crisis" to audit your system is not a good idea. It is far easier to take control of your system when technically proficient people who have worked on it are available. This virtually eliminates the time-consuming "sleuthing" aspect of the audit.

Why Audit?

Systems should be audited for several different reasons (see Figure 1.1):

1. To control system resources unknown to the auditor. The "Monday morning" case.

2. To verify the operation of a known system. Hopefully, this is how you'll do your first audit.

3. To measure the impact of a planned revision or change of a known system.

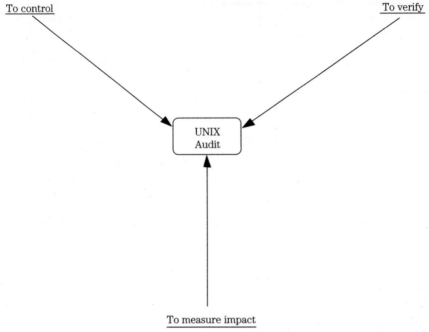

Figure 1.1 Why audit?

Production systems in particular are crucial corporate resources. An important objective of the corporation is to control its resources so they are not squandered. Another important objective is to see that these resources are used in an optimal fashion to achieve the mission for which they were acquired.

Remember when you first purchased that computer? You probably had to justify the expense as well as the cost of ownership. Now that the system has been in production, what measures are in place to ensure that the *system resource* is performing as expected?

UNIX in Particular

Whether because of UNIX's origins, or how it was made available to the marketplace, or how the planets were positioned over the original authors, UNIX has gotten off to a bumpy start. In the early 1980s, a number of software development companies and MIS departments switched to UNIX when it was first made available on "super micros," as they were called. Most of these "early adapters" saw great benefits to using UNIX. They were able to break the proprietary hold of major computer manufacturers. They were impressed by the functional richness and comprehensive tool set offered by UNIX. Of course, it didn't hurt that the cost of

UNIX was so low (less than $1,000, or bundled in with the hardware, making it look free). Most of these companies were convinced that the UNIX operating system would dominate the market within a few years. That didn't happen.

The UNIX that entered the marketplace in the early 1980s left you on your own with poor documentation and not too many places to go for help. UNIX was as much a cult as it was a body of software. Or better still, UNIX was to computing what "peace and love" was to the 1960s. Lots of people were "rolling their own."

The consequence of all this "democracy" was a lot of know-how and a lot of chaos. Companies that purchased UNIX-based systems for price alone soon discovered that the cost savings they expected to realize was more than offset by the programming costs required to build software that wasn't available at that time. Tried-and-true commercial office and application products abundantly available on proprietary systems were simply not available on early UNIX platforms. In the early years, UNIX-based platforms were reasonable choices for those companies that had to create lots of custom software or had to use scientific products.

Think about it. Corporate buyers and advisors (MIS departments or their consultants) had to now consider hardware and software combinations that were one-third or one-fourth the cost of the proprietary system they'd normally buy. While these new systems were long on power and low on cost, they were sold by a new breed of corporate supplier, the *OEM* (original equipment manufacturer) or, more commonly, the *VAR* (value-added reseller). On average, these suppliers were technically stronger and more focused on the buyer's application needs than the traditional corporate suppliers. They lacked, however, the financial strength (OEMs and VARs were usually very small firms) and the lifecycle support services provided by the traditional suppliers.

In both the buyer's and the supplier's firms, early UNIX developers were notorious for "clever" renditions of software. The plain fact is that most software developers lacked the business savvy required to field a well-supported development effort or product. There was a real need to control these new software developers without suppressing their creativity. These developers were typically scientists or engineers to whom "cryptic" did not mean "unfriendly"; it simply meant less typing was required.

Today, the lack of commercial office and application software is no longer a problem. As we move through the second decade of commercially available UNIX, never has so much cost so little, and struck so much terror, in the hearts of suppliers of proprietary operating systems. In recent years, with the widespread use of UNIX, we have learned that to be commercially viable, UNIX required significantly more support and control than its earlier scientific beginnings foresaw. For that reason, auditing a UNIX system is a practical control and support activity.

The Right Approach

No audit will succeed without the right approach to gaining information. If you are an outside auditor, you might well be viewed as a threat by an existing MIS group or one or more sets of system users. On the other hand, you might be welcomed as an independent professional skilled at interpreting objective evidence—someone who will not only improve the lot of all system users, but who will leave methods and procedures in place that can be used for years to come.

Whether you are an outside auditor or a responsible company manager, you have a selling job on your hands. This sales effort should take the form of gentle persuasion that emphasizes your *helping* role, and de-emphasizes your report to management. If you are an outside consultant or a staff professional, you should follow these steps:

1. Before assuming an auditing assignment, be sure to explain and assure all participants that your findings will not be used as a "club" or recrimination of past failings or omissions.

2. Begin your audit by making a presentation to all of the key participants, asking for their help. Tell them about these specific features of your audit:
   —Benefits
   —Common misperceptions
   —Your mission
   —Methods you will use
   —Estimates of typical or average findings
   —Time it will take
   —Who should be involved
   —Typical audit recommendations
   —Schedule of events

3. Explain any handouts (such as questionnaires or lists of audit topics) to key management *before* distributing them.

4. Ask for everything you will need in writing before getting underway. A system audit is similar to an accounting audit in that you can only assess information made available to you. As an auditor, you need to demonstrate *due diligence* in case information is inadvertently or purposely not provided.

5. Determine the context of your audit. That is, define the corporate culture, the demands made on both users and system administrators, how well-funded the MIS effort has been to date, and so on.

6. Get a company liaison assigned to open doors that need to be opened or to handle all of the scheduling of people and resources you will need.

Audit Preplanning

You don't want to do an audit without a plan. Your audit should have specific goals and objectives which will influence your audit methods, techniques and time it takes to accomplish. So what should the audit plan consist of?

Don't get bogged down in detail without knowing why and unless there is a good reason. Look for the obvious. Don't develop an audit report without addressing the obvious. The first basics you should attend to are these:

1. *Talk to system users.* Talking to system users is starting with the obvious. If the system you are auditing lacks data or functional integrity, or is too slow or has run out of room or is restricting its users in any way, they will tell you. Talking to users will not help if they are not using the system. This happens when users are not properly trained or the system is so bad that people have abandoned it.

2. *Read company reports or memos regarding the system, its software, and any related services.* Someone might have documented the problems people are talking to you about. If documentation does exist, be sure it contains all aspects of the problem(s): descriptions, symptoms, and causes.

3. *Interview the system administrator.* The person who should know the current state of the system best, as well as its historical development, is the system administrator.

4. *If possible, interview the original company purchaser or purchasing group.* Don't let the fact that they might have left the company stop you. If they have left on good terms, contact them at their current employment and conduct a telephone interview.

5. *Review the original purchase order and terms of sale.* Many times the original purchasing paperwork reveals information about what was purchased or purchasing terms that explain current findings. These can be anything from illegal licensing, to missing products, to services never rendered. Many purchase orders that are issued are done on a conditional basis. These conditions are often overlooked immediately after initial installation.

6. *Review all purchases of products and services made after the system was installed.* The same conditions that are true in the last item can be true here. Or perhaps additional or corrective purchase orders were issued and products arrived but were never installed. This is a frequent occurrence after systems are in production. An order is received after the original requester has left the company and the product is set on a shelf and never installed.

7. *Review all hardware and software maintenance agreements.* Here too, warranties and guarantees of service for both hardware and software need to be reviewed to ensure they are in full force and effect.

8. *Review all system logs and any procedure manuals developed during the years of operations.* Good practice dictates that the system administrator keep both a chronological system log (like the captain of a ship) and an organized procedure manual that contains every official system procedure practiced at this site.

9. *Review the disaster recovery plan as well as the results of any tests or uses of the plan.* Disaster recovery plans are generally a soft spot at most installations. If one exists, it's probably untried.

The results of these interviews and reviews will determine what needs simple verification and what needs more in-depth scrutiny.

Not All Audits Are the Same

Your overall approach to the audit will depend on the circumstances surrounding the audit and the staff that is available to assist you. The table below describes the possibilities.

Audit circumstances	Technical staff help	User staff help	Outside support	No outside support
Routine	1	5	9	13
Upgrade	2	6	10	14
First	3	7	11	15
Emergency	4	8	12	16

The easiest audit to conduct is a routine audit with competent help at the system site. The most difficult audit is an emergency audit conducted with no on-site help on a system that no longer has operating system support.

The Right Audit at the Right Time

When you do an audit you can spell the difference between a "cake walk" and a difficult ordeal. It is best to establish good audit practices at the beginning stages of a system's life.

Audit procedures and intervals should be set based on the stage of system life you are at. Your involvement at each stage is essential. As shown in Figure 1.2, there are five stages that need to be considered:

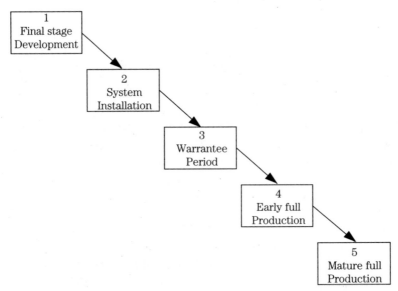

Figure 1.2 The stages of system evolution.

1. *Final stage of development.*   If you're a manager, you might be tempted to avoid getting involved until the "new system" is installed. That's a mistake. Don't miss the opportunity to attend any number of presentations (such as initial user training, user functional acceptance, and system administration training).

   Pre-audit activities are appropriate during this stage. These consist of learning enough about the system to have measurable expectations once production begins. For example, you might learn all of the functional aspects of the system along with application users during their training and acceptance of developed modules. This is an ideal stage for such activities because the original system designers and authors of the software are present. Your presence can and should influence better and more comprehensive documentation.

2. *System installation.*   The ideal first audit should be executed at the end of stage 2, system installation. This should be the *baseline audit* for system tracking through all subsequent stages. You might be tempted to rush the system into production if its development is late, as are many installations. A detailed file system definition as well as system parameter documentation is most easily captured at this stage mainly because the system builders are still available and there is current knowledge about your system.

   Measurements of file systems should be made before and after initial data loading or conversion of data from other systems onto this one.

3. *Warranteed production period.* Assuming your warranteed production period is one year long, you should audit the system's performance on a quarterly basis. Most of your findings will be functional issues caused by inexact matches between needs and programmed functions, functional requirements learned after the installation, or software errors and omissions. Early problems will consist of software errors, resource-sharing conflicts, and operating tuning issues. Remember that this transition from development to production is the period of greatest change.

4. *Full production—rapid growth phase.* By the end of the first year of use, functional related issues will be under control. However, the rate of data growth is usually still expanding. New volume breakpoints that application or operating system software might not take in stride are being reached. Also, most significant enhancements are being added during this time as a response to using and understanding the software that was originally delivered.

5. *Full steady state production.* With few exceptions, after the first few years of operation the purge/archive cycles catch up with rapid data growth, and the system settles down to regular and predictable operations. Problems related to data volume changes are less likely. This period is characterized by very stable operations with most procedures automated or made highly routine.

These five stages cover the entire span of a system's life from preinstallation to full and mature production use. Audits performed during these stages have different purposes and require different audit procedures.

Audit Roles

The system audit is a participatory activity. The major players are the system "owner," the system users, and the auditor(s).

System owner

The owner is usually the executive who funds the audit on behalf of the corporation. This can be a corporate executive from general management or from the company's MIS group itself. Sometimes, the owner is an outsider interested in evaluating the MIS function as a whole in order to evaluate and purchase the company. The following issues are important to owners:

1. *Am I at risk?* This is a bottom-line question from someone who has delegated all system-related functions to others. It's a question posed by someone to simply determine if everything's "okay." The answer to this question will determine if the corporation needs to buy more technology

or know-how as insurance against the loss of valuable information or day-to-day functionality.

2. *Am I getting my money's worth?*   If the corporation is paying too much for the current technical capabilities, what are the alternatives?

3. *Can I do better?*   Should I make further investments in information technology? If so, what should they be?

4. *How am I positioned for the next few years?*   Are there problems foreseen by the audit that we can get minimized by acting now? Is my corporation foregoing opportunities because of shortsighted economics?

Applications users

System users fall into two categories: application users (businesspeople, end users) and MIS users (support or technical users). The following issues are important to application users:

1. *Does the system meet my needs?*   If the system is not appropriate, or addresses needs not pertinent or helpful, users will be unabashed about their discontent.

2. *Is the system reliable?*   The system might be functionally correct, but do these functions work completely and consistently under all circumstances?

3. *Is the system easy to use?*   If the necessary and reliable functions are present, are they too difficult to learn how to use? Are they cumbersome? Is the workflow wrong?

4. *Is the system available when I need to use it?*   All other things being acceptable, is the system functionally accessible by those who need it, when they need it?

5. *Is the system fast enough?*   Is the interactive response rapid enough not to reduce the workflow effectiveness demanded by the users?

6. *Is the system secure?*   Can the system be accessed from a remote location via LAN or WAN bridges or gateways, or by remote dial in?

MIS users

The following issues are important to MIS users:

1. *Is their enough resource to meet user needs?*   Is the hardware and software in place to adequately meet the needs of the application user community?

2. *Can the MIS staff withstand the departure of key employees?*   Are the key technical personnel backed up by "understudies," outside resources, documentation, methods, and procedures?

3. *Can functional access be permitted while retaining security?* Systems that are used by many people and accessed by other computers must balance network connectivity and openness with restricted and authorized access.

4. *Can the organization withstand a system failure?* Is there a disaster/recovery plan in place? Has it been tested?

5. *Should the operating system software be upgraded?* Do the release notes of the next version of the operating system offer sufficient fixes or enhancements to justify the upgrade effort? Are upgrades to other software products forcing an operating system upgrade?

Auditor

Auditor's issues are the same whether the auditor is an "outside expert" or a manager in your company. These are as follows:

1. *Is there access to all of the system information necessary to conduct the audit?* Has access to all pertinent company records been made available?

2. *Has an accurate baseline measurement been established in the past?* If not, what are the chances of executing a base-level reinstallation of the production system?

3. *Have accurate measurements been taken during the current audit?* Were measurements taken under controlled conditions?

4. *Have the audit results been correctly analyzed and then synthesized?* Can the new measurements be explained in light of the last benchmark? Have new measurements been taken that reflect a resequencing of tests suggested by the results of initial interviews and tests?

5. *Have both risk and cost benefits been prepared based on the recommended execution of the action item list?*

The Bigger Audit Picture

The remainder of this book pursues various details of audit mechanics based on circumstances, available support, and the stage of a system's maturity. It is helpful to understand the underlying audit basics, consisting of the following:

- Examining
- Reviewing
- Reporting
- Recommending

Auditor	Investigator
Examine	Discover
Review	Analyze
Report	Conclude
Recommend	Action

Figure 1.3 The auditor and the investigator: similar roles in pursuing evidence.

These basics are applied over and over again throughout this book by topics that are system-specific and UNIX-specific.

As shown in Figure 1.3, these components are analogous to those required by investigators to uncover and document evidence:

- Discovery
- Analysis
- Conclusion
- Action plan

As you continue to explore this book, be mindful of the commonsense approach to auditing. Some details recommended here might not be appropriate to your needs. Feel free to distinguish the underlying basic "audit components" and rearrange procedural steps to better meet your specific situation.

2

Audit Plan Deliverable

The audit plan, like the methodology, can either be a real help in attaining your audit goals, or it can provide you with a false sense of security. Remember, the *plan* is not the *audit*. To be effective, the plan must be customized and adapted for each specific audit. Understanding the plan as a guide or reference to a norm as opposed to a rigid set of procedures will ensure that your planning doesn't get in your way.

Chapter 1 pointed out that there should be different plans for the different situations. This chapter describes the form and content of the written audit plan deliverable. It suggests the outline of each of two separate documents as well as a detailed description of their contents for doing a comprehensive audit. Of course, the documents should be modified, depending on what type of audit you are conducting.

The contents of the documents define the audit plan components that will make sense in most audit procedures. The motive and purpose for each component will be discussed.

Design the Report First

The final deliverable of any plan is an audit report. The deliverable *is not* a better system, a controlled system, an optimized system. Actually using the information from the audit is not up to you and should have no bearing on the report's contents.

The report should be organized in a journalistic, top-down fashion. In general terms, the audit report should have the following organization:

1. Audit abstract

2. Action items

3. Methodology used

4. Findings

5. Conclusions

Only the first two items would be presented to executive management. Those needing to understand the why's and how's of the action items and the audit itself would read items 3, 4, and 5.

The *report* is the audit deliverable. The audit's activities, as numerous and lengthy as they might be, come and go. The remaining report, however, is the basis for any future action and benefit that proceeds from the audit.

You will make your auditing job a lot easier if you have the outline of a report in mind when you start the audit, because audit activities can be very fragmenting. They can draw you into numerous side issues having little to do with the original audit mission. The report outline will, of course, depend on how you design your audit plan. Think of the report as the deliverable for the audit, and the report outline as the deliverable for the audit plan.

The entire audit report should be delivered as two separate but related documents. The first document, the *executive report*, should be presented to the owner or the highest level of executive authority. The following is a suggested outline for this report:

I. Executive report
   A. Audit abstract
      1. Summary judgment
      2. Summary recommendation
      3. Summary cost
      4. Summary benefit
   B. Action items
      1. Action items in order of priority
      2. Action plan in order of implementation
      3. Schedule of action plan
      4. Cost of each step in the action plan
      5. Short- and long-term benefit

The second document, the *management report*, should be presented to the company's operating or line management. This document represents the "meat and potatoes" of the audit. It contains enough detail for management to probe further or pursue any additional research they might deem appropriate. The following is a suggested outline for this report:

II. Management report
   A. Methodology used

1. Audit mission
2. Audit documents
3. Audit interviews
4. Audit equipment
5. Audit security
6. Audit file system
7. Audit software
8. Audit network access
9. Audit performance
10. Audit system administration
11. Audit disaster recovery plan

B. Findings
1. Record of measurements
2. Comparison to baseline
3. Baseline rollover

C. Conclusions
1. Interpreting the results
2. Suggested research
3. Benefits and costs of recommendations

Executive Report Details

The executive report caters to the busy executive who needs to know final results rather than "how things got that way." This report assumes its conclusions are fully correct and well supported. It is brief, action-oriented, and leaves the details to its companion, the management report.

The executive report is organized into two brief segments. The first segment is a one-page summary of the entire audit, its results, conclusions, and recommendations, including a summary of costs and benefits. The second segment is a summary extract of the conclusions section of the management report.

Audit abstract

The abstract summarizes your judgments and recommendations resulting from the audit examination and review. The writing style is exclusively declarative. It is never conditional or waffling. You address your responsibilities as auditor by stating a clear, unequivocal judgment in executive terms. This assessment is then followed by a summary of recommendations.

Next, a summarized cost estimate of the audit's recommendations should be stated. And finally, the estimated benefit, in financial terms, should be stated along with the ROI (Return On Investment) if the recommendations are followed. Examples of these abstract components follow.

Case 1 example. *Summary judgment.* The audit revealed no material problems that require action at this time.

Summary recommendation. I recommend that you upgrade your operating system so that you can realize benefits resulting from enhancements to other products you already own. Furthermore, I have instructed your staff to confirm the growth of data on one of your systems; its growth is exceeding baseline predictions.

Summary cost. The total cost of following this audit's recommendations is estimated to be $12,000.

Summary benefit. By enhancing existing products you will satisfy the requests of two departments for custom-built solutions. This will result in a tangible saving of $35,000 within six months, and an intangible improvement in service to your customers.

Case 1 discussion. Did someone say "short"? Yes, it is short. But if that's the result of the audit, that's all you need to say. Don't be compelled to deliver tonnage unless you have a need to demonstrate insecurity. The substance of your efforts will be evident from the management report that will be delivered at the same time. Your due diligence will be obvious to anyone who cares to read it, including the chief executive.

The summary judgment you have rendered is sound and is based on current evidence and predictable trends. The recommendations consist of a recognized opportunity and the need to correct an unnecessary use of disk space by one segment of the user community. Ah! You didn't mention that the use is unnecessary! That's right. You have judged that the issue is explainable and the staff has agreed to archive information that is not required online. All that matters in the abstract is that the executive be made aware that instructions need to be followed.

The summary cost is stated in absolute terms. The cost includes both "hard" costs (outside dollars) and "soft" costs (inside dollars). Gross costs associated with each step will be listed in the action items section of this report. All details, including cash flow analysis, will be provided in the management report.

The summary benefit should be conservative and stick only to what can be readily measured. In addition to this, it is reasonable to allude to intangible benefits, but avoid making judgments as to their value. You're an auditor, not a prophet. Executives are surrounded by others who practice the art of "reading tea leaves." Leave the intangible "guesstimates" to them.

Case 2 example. *Summary judgment.* The audit report revealed a serious exposure that needs to be addressed immediately.

Summary recommendation. I recommend that you replace your current computer system and migrate all of your software and data as soon as possible. As it is, your system has no hardware or software maintenance agreements since the original supplier went out of business. Your current staff has kept this system operational for years. Essential to their efforts has been the cooperation and support provided by the computer manufacturer. Since the last audit, the manufacturer's support is no longer available. Your aggressive rate of growth and planned expansions are all at considerable risk if your current system is unavailable due to any extended outage.

Summary cost. The total cost of this recommendation is estimated to be $180,000. Your outside cost of ownership will be approximately $3,000 per year. The total cost will be used to replace the central portion of the hardware (computer, disks, and backup unit). External peripherals (terminals, printers, modems, and 9-track tape) can and will be reused.

Summary benefit. The recommendation will move you to a supported system that is more reliable than your current system, and which can be repaired in less than a day in the event of failure.

Case 2 discussion.   The summary judgment is serious. It is meant to get attention. The first sentence states the summary recommendation clearly and succinctly. The remainder of the summary recommendation discusses the main reasons for that recommendation due to the significant change it calls for. The summary cost also provides further explanations due to the size of the anticipated expense.

The summary benefit, while real, is very intangible. It is a benefit that is measured against what might happen. This benefit is truly about business insurance. While it is true that a newer system might perform faster, improve productivity, and be easier to manage, the primary motive for the recommendation is stated. Further benefits just mentioned may be used by others to help justify the cost of an unplanned expenditure or these might be side benefits of a must-do business decision.

Action items

The action items section is similar to the abstract in that it is a concise summary. Action items flesh out what needs to be done. This section puts substance to the recommendation and cost section stated in the abstract. It answers the question, "How will we get where we need to be and what will it cost?"

This section starts out by listing the main planning segments required to achieve the recommendations in order of their importance. It then lists implementation steps in chronological order for each planning segment. Calendar time estimates (not elapsed time) and dependencies for each planning segment are proposed for the reader's review and consideration.

Each step along with its proposed schedule is cost-estimated along with any long- or short-term benefit that will be realized.

Case 1, for instance, would have no action items section. Case 2, on the other hand, would have a lengthy action items section.

Case 2 example

I. Planning segments
    A. Equipment purchases
    B. Software purchases
    C. Conversion services

II. Implementation steps
    A. Equipment purchases
       1. Size current equipment
       2. Project three to five year growth (if any)
       3. Issue RFI
       4. Evaluate what is available
       5. Issue RFP
       6. Evaluate
       7. Issue purchase order
       8. Install equipment
       9. Test installation
    B. Software purchases
       1. Identify system software and layered products currently in use
       2. Identify any version incompatibilities
       3. Purchase upgraded products
       4. Install and test upgrades
    C. Conversion services
       1. Unload data onto common media
       2. Read data from old system onto new system
       3. Reformat data if required by new hardware or upgraded software
       4. Upload data into application directories and/or databases
       5. Retrain system administrator(s)
       6. Test fully loaded application systems
       7. Release to Production

Estimates, dependencies, costs. All three planning segments can begin at the same time. Software purchases and conversion services, however, must lag behind until equipment purchases are complete. The time and costs required for each planning segment is as follows:

- Equipment purchases: two months, $85,000
- Software purchases: one month, $15,000
- Conversion services: one month, $80,000

The total calendar time for an integrated project will be three months. There are no intermediate short-term benefits to be realized. The first and primary benefit is the full integrated repositioning at the end of system replacement.

Case 2 discussion. Planning segments declare what needs to be done in the simplest of terms.

Implementation steps describe one level of detail for each of the planning segments. The list of chronological steps are intended to define the planning segment's activities.

The section on estimates, dependencies, and costs focuses on the time, costs, and coordination of the action items to be successful. There is no attempt to justify or explain the reasons for any specific cost. These details, including time and cost alternatives that were reviewed, will be presented in the management report.

Management Report Details

The management report is a detailed record of the audit as it was carried out. Depending on the circumstances of the audit, it might qualify as a replacement for the last audit's baseline. The report consists of a fixed and variable portion of audit details. The fixed portion is the *methodology*, which is usually defined at the beginning of system ownership and does not change very much throughout the system's life. Fixed measurement techniques must be employed in order to benefit from monitoring aspect of the findings from audit to audit over various system growth stages.

The variable portion of the audit is the *findings*. This section is primarily tabular. The findings section is where the actual measurements from the current audit are recorded. Furthermore, in this section you can view the measurements taken during the last audit. Finally, this section discusses the disposition of these measurements and whether they qualify as new baseline readings.

The management's report *conclusion* section interprets the findings in the last section, as well as the variance if an older baseline is involved. The conclusion might call for an applications-oriented research study beyond the scope of the system audit just concluded. This section details what needs to be done and proposes alternatives.

Methodology

The methodology section of the report describes what was audited and how it was audited. It contains 11 sections.

Mission. The methodology section starts with a definition of the audit's mission. As mentioned in chapter 1, an audit will be carried out for different reasons and under different circumstances on systems in one of the five stages of life. The mission section documents the conditions and stage of the audited system.

Documents. The next section documents what records to review and what specifically to look for. This task is usually substantial at the first audit and insignificant thereafter.

Documents that should be audited once include the following:

- System's RFP
- System's proposal
- System's quotation
- Purchase order (contract)
- Hardware maintenance agreement(s)
- Software maintenance agreement(s)

Documents that should be reviewed at each audit include the following:

- Added purchase and maintenance agreements since previous audit
- System log since last audit
- System procedures since last audit
- Relevant correspondence

Interviews. The interviews section documents who you interviewed and what the purpose of the interviews were. Common observations and perceptions from the interviews should be at the top of your list of findings.

Equipment. Configuration details should be described in detail. The full system including the topology of the network it may be connected to needs to be documented.

Security. The security section provides a full report on the system's security. It discusses all aspects of security including physical access, logical access, functional access, data access, remote access, and network access.

File system. The file system needs to be reported on at a number of levels. Reporting against the operating system's distribution is first. That is, what is loaded from the original distribution and what is not? The purpose is to find out that what is loaded is identical to the latest distribution in the company's possession.

The rest of the file system will either contain programs and data or be free and available for storage. The audit should report on what is there, why it is there, and how it is used.

Software. A strict definition of UNIX would include the kernel and very little more. The majority of what is loosely considered UNIX is really a collection of UNIX utilities and ancillary programs. Consider, though, that the UNIX kernel and device drivers take up two to three megabytes while the remainder of the utilities take approximately 35 to 50 megabytes. Recent UNIX versions that include "X" software, "soft fonts," and network software can occupy as much as 150 megabytes.

Many UNIX system owners do not load the full set of UNIX extensions. You as auditor should measure just how much operating system software is loaded versus what is actually needed. You can run application software with as little as 15 MBs, while a fully loaded set of extensions can bring the operating system software distribution to 150 MBs.

Next, system tool software needs to be accounted for. That is, what compilers, editors, and system administration software is on the system? Other software products like database management software and 4GLs (fourth generation languages) also need to be measured and accounted for.

Network access. As advertisers tell us, "The network is the system." The topology of the network needs to be fully mapped. Each system's purpose and access rights need to be reported on.

Performance. The keystones of user happiness are software functionality and interactive system response. Initial test measurements will indicate whether extensive performance measurements need to be taken. UNIX has extensive performance measurement tools. The only caution is that the measurements be made under controlled conditions.

System administration. UNIX is a timesharing system that requires a certain amount of "care and feeding" to manage resource usage. Methods, procedures, and practice documentation need to be audited.

Disaster recovery. Is there a written plan? Are responsibilities assigned? Are action items spelled out in detail? Does the plan rely exclusively on key employees? Has the plan ever been tested? Are there UNIX-specific issues that need to be addressed? These are the pertinent contents of disaster recovery.

Findings

Separating what is found from the methodology used to examine the system will make it easier to present the results of the measurements, regardless of the methodology used. The findings section should be the official "record of measurements" for this audit. Furthermore, it is here that comparisons to any previous baselines should be recorded and commented on.

Finally, a decision as to whether to roll over the baseline to this current audit should be recorded here. If the current audit was the periodic audit, then the baseline should be rolled, and that should be simply stated. On the other hand, the measurements taken in this audit might not be sufficient for a complete baseline report. If this is true, the auditor should point out what activities are appropriate to roll the baseline so that a decision can be made.

Conclusions

The last section should contain conclusions with reasoned interpretations. Using the measurements of the audit, comparisons to baseline, interviews with line and management personnel, and a review of future plans, you must "make your case." Your knowledge and experience are brought to bear on the evidence presented as the audit's findings. Conclusions drawn from the interpretation of all of the factors mentioned should be dispassionate and have no regard for cost or organizational consequence.

If the audit has been limited by necessity or budget, suggestions for further research might be appropriate. Further research might also be suggested based on tentative business plans that are being budgeted for at the time of the audit.

In the strictest sense, the audit is complete once it presents and interprets its findings. If you are an experienced system-level professional, you should make the final recommendations resulting in action items to be used in an implementation plan. If you are more of a diligent business manager, now is the time to seek someone with both professional system and business experience.

The scientific- and evidence-driven review should conclude with a cost/benefit analysis of the auditor's recommendations.

3

Prerequisites

The minimum prerequisites to do a UNIX audit are the following:

- Management experience and skills
- General computer literacy
- Good verbal and written communication skills

The ideal prerequisites are the minimum ones plus the following:

- Audit experience
- UNIX literacy
- System integration experience and knowledge

There is no reason why a manager with no UNIX background cannot audit a UNIX System. Ideally, such a manager will reduce the time it takes and smooth the learning curve if he teams up with a technician who works in UNIX on a regular basis (such as a system administrator or a system programmer).

If you're going it alone you need to know the following:

- How to log onto the system
- The root password
- Basic file structure information
- The vi editor
- UNIX commands that can be used for auditing

Most of this information is readily available in any number of UNIX primers. In my opinion, the best primer is *Introducing the UNIX System* by Henry McGilton and Rachel Morgan, originally published by McGraw-Hill (1983). You will not have to master the primer before doing the audit. Budget approximately 15 hours of reading to cover the basic principles. Spend another six hours practicing basic vi to both create and modify short text files.

Be aware of popular rumors about UNIX, such as how cryptic it is. Or how hard the vi editor is to use. It is true that, compared to some other operating systems, UNIX is cryptic, and vi is not a "kind" or "obvious" product. Unadorned UNIX suffers from its historic roots in the early 1970s when interactive users were limited by 10 characters-per-second hardcopy teletypes and when most users were scientists and engineers, not typists. To them, cryptic cp was much more desirable than friendly "COPY." The commands you will use, or the amount of vi you will have to type, will not require extraordinary effort on your part.

The remainder of this chapter briefly explains the UNIX file structure. It identifies, organizes, and explains commands that can be used to audit UNIX. Remember, however, that the purpose of this text is not to teach you UNIX. It is to show you how to use resources native to UNIX to examine a UNIX-based system.

UNIX File Structure

The UNIX file structure, like MS-DOS, is hierarchical. Directories contain files. Files can contain either data or programs. *Structure* refers to how directories are organized. They cascade down, so to speak, from a main directory called *root* to many *subdirectories*.

From an auditor's point of view, some directory structures are standard in any UNIX distribution. As UNIX versions continue to standardize, this UNIX *distribution* (the set of UNIX software received from the computer manufacturer or third party) will be identical except for optional extensions.

Before going further with the audit, be sure to review your UNIX primer's section that describes file structures and defines the following:

- Root directory
- Home directory
- Pathnames
- Directory navigation commands: cd, pwd

Your primer should also have a diagram of a traditional UNIX software distribution directory.

UNIX Commands

The remainder of this chapter focuses on 74 UNIX commands, out of approximately 250 possible commands. If you're new to UNIX, this will limit the scope of things you might want to learn about in order to audit UNIX. You will learn how to use UNIX commands to answer resource utilization questions about those functions or information that you, your company, or your client's company have entrusted to a UNIX-based computer system.

The two sections that follow deal with UNIX commands that are particularly useful to an auditor. The first section organizes applicable commands by grouping them into meaningful categories. The second section describes and gives an example use of each command that you can try out at a terminal. All commands except **vi** are essentially read-only commands.

Sixty-three of the 74 commands are available to general users and are completely defined in the *UNIX Users Reference Manual.* The remaining 11 commands are available to system administrators and are fully defined in the *UNIX Administration Manual.* If you are logged on as **root** or **sysadm** you should have permission to use all of these commands.

Commands organized by use

To better understand and remember the commands, it is helpful to organize them by how they are likely to be used in an audit.

The 74 commands that would likely be used in an audit fall into the following six categories:

- Commands that do general *administration*
- Commands to inspect *file* systems
- Commands to inspect *network* facilities
- Commands to examine *performance*
- Commands to examine *security*
- Commands that serve as general *utility* tools

Some commands fall into more than one group. Commands are listed under each category of use.

Administration

Command	Access	Command	Access
captoinfo	admin	kill	user
df	admin	lpstat	user
fuser	admin	man	user
groups	user	nice	user

Administration

Command	Access	Command	Access
nohup	user	sysadm	admin
pack	user	sysdef	admin
pr	user	systemid	admin
ps	user	uname	user
su	user	uucheck	admin
sum	user	whodo	admin

File

Command	Access	Command	Access
bfs	user	fuser	admin
checkmm	user	ls	user
cmp	user	od	user
cpio	user	pack	user
df	admin	pr	user
diff, bdiff	user	strings	user
diffmk	user	sum	user
du	user	tail	user
env	user	tar	user
file	user	umask	user
find	user	vi, view	user

Network

Command	Access	Command	Access
ct	user	uustat	user
cu	user		

Performance

Command	Access	Command	Access
acctcom	user	renice	user
at	user	sa1, sa2, sadc	admin
nice	user		

Security

Command	Access	Command	Access
acctcom	user	diffmk	user
chmod	user	find	user
ct	user	groups	user
cu	user	last	user
diff, bdiff	user	newgrp	user
pwck, grpck	admin	sum	user
su	user	umask	user

Utility

Command	Access	Command	Access
at	user	man	user
bcs_cat	admin	mkdir	user
bfs	user	more, page	user
captoinfo	admin	nice	user
cat	user	nohup	user
cd	user	od	user
clear	user	ps	user
cp, mv	user	pwd	user
cpio	user	renice	user
crontab	user	rm, rmdir	user
csplit	user	script	user
cut	user	sleep	user
date	user	sort	user
dd	user	sum	user
df	admin	sysadm	admin
diff, bdiff	user	tail	user
diffmk	user	tar	user
du	user	tee	user
echo	user	time, timex	user
env	user	unique	user
file	user	vi, view	user
find	user	wc	user
grep	user	who	user
head	user		

Alphabetical reference

The previous section grouped commands by how they might be used in an audit. This section is strictly a reference. Its purpose is to allow you to explore and learn about each of these UNIX commands that are used later in this book as "audit tools."

This section comments on each of the 74 commands in alphabetical order. Each command is named, followed by the term *user* or *admin* to designate which type of command access is required. The command is then described and commented on. Certain options judged to have specific audit value are named. Sometimes, examples or samples of information provided by the command accompanies the comments.

These commands were available and tested on an Aviion workstation, manufactured by Data General using a System-V-compliant UNIX designed to run on Motorola's 88000 RISC architecture. Some of these commands might not be available on the UNIX systems you audit.

acctcom (user). Use the `acctcom` command to show a comprehensive list containing information about each command issued by any user. For each command issued, the list contains the command name, user ID, the terminal at which the command was issued, start and end times, and elapsed time.

This command is one of many system accounting commands available. This particular command is used to analyze the detail log of all commands that were issued for the day. It should be used to analyze detailed system history for a known time interval. That is, if you want to know exactly who was doing what at 10:22 a.m. today, the output from this command will tell you.

An example of `acctcom` output follows:

```
Command                  Start     End      Real    CPU       Mean
name     User  Ttyname  time      (secs)   (secs)  size(K)
rm       adm   tty02    10:22:02  10:22:02  0.22    0.10      0.00
sh       root  tty05    10:22:04  10:22:05  1.06    0.14     11.00
sdac     sys   ?        10:22:07  10:22:07  0.38    0.18     21.00
```

at (user). The `at` command provides a convenient way to run a specific measurement command file at a specific time designated by you. For example, it might be critical that you run a batch performance test at an inconvenient time; this command will do it for you.

This command is always used in conjunction with other commands or batch command files (shell scripts). It allows you to start up a command or batch command file at an absolute time in the future or at a relative time from now.

Type in the following command lines to see how this command can be useful:

```
at now + 5 minutes [Enter]
ls -l / [Enter]
[Ctrl-d]
#
```

Five minutes from now, the system will display the root directory's long listing on your terminal.

An example of starting up a batch command file called "mybatch" with this command follows:

```
at -f mybatch now + 5 minutes [Enter]
#
```

bcs_cat (admin). Use `bcs_cat` to print current system and network information known to your system at your terminal: type of hosts, networks, passwords, protocols, group, or service information.

This command offers you a noninvasive form of report which looks in the "etc" directory for the type of file specified. For example, the following shows the command issued from any directory to obtain group information for a UNIX system, with its typical output:

```
#bcs_cat group [Enter]

root::0:root
other::1:
bin::2:root,bin,daemon
sys::3:root,bin,sys,adm
adm::4:root,adm,daemon
mail::5:mail,bin
lp::6:lp
uucp::8:uucp
daemon::12:root,daemon
operator::18:adm
nfs::38:nfs
ftp::39:ftp
general::100:
#
```

bfs (user). Use the **bfs** command to scan very large text files ("Big File Scan") in order to reduce the files to editable components using a **csplit** command.

captoinfo (admin). Use **captoinfo** to view terminal and printer characteristic definitions.

If users are complaining about not being able to use all of the features they know are possible with their terminals, then this is the command to use to see how UNIX understands the terminal type's characteristics.

cat (user). Use **cat** to concatenate (combine) files together or to append information at the end of a text file.

This command displays text files to a video display screen. One of the most useful options to the **cat** command is the **–v** option, which prints nonprinting characters.

cd (user). Use **cd** to change working directories.

You will use this command over and over to move from one directory to another. When naming files you have two choices: to use the full "pathname" or to use the file's "base name." If you know you are going to be issuing many commands on files in the same directory, it would be wise to move there and make it your working directory.

checkmm (user). Use checkmm to check for files formatted to use the mm, mmt, eqn, neqn, and tbl macros.

This command comes in handy if the system being audited makes extensive use of the mm macro in conjunction with **nroff** or **troff** formatters.

chmod (user). The chmod command changes the security mode of a file by changing its user access rights by type of user. It should only be used to change access permissions on files you create.

clear (user). The clear command clears your terminal screen. It is a simple utility command to get a "fresh start" at your terminal.

cmp (user). The cmp command compares two files. Use it to print details of the difference between two files (if there are differences). The following shows a typical use and its output:

```
#cmp test1 test2

test1 test2 differ: char 20, line 2
#
```

cp, mv (user). Use cp or mv to copy or move files from one file and/or directory to another.

This command is a basic copy or move utility. Be careful not to move (mv) any files that you didn't create.

cpio (user). The cpio command copies file archives onto or from disk. This is a powerful utility generally used to copy or restore sets of files and directories to or from removable media. Use this command to manage benchmark sets of system files.

crontab (user). Compared to the at command, crontab provides a more permanent way to repeat certain operations at predetermined times on a regular basis.

To gain access to this function, your name must be found in the following file:

```
/usr/lib/cron/cron.allow
```

and must not be present in this file:

```
/usr/lib/cron/cron.deny
```

For example, if you wanted to run the same performance measure each hour between 8 a.m. and 7 p.m. on Mondays, Wednesdays, and Fridays, you would make a few entries in `crontab`.

csplit (user). The `csplit` command does a context split on a large text file.

UNIX editors have size restrictions when it comes to very large files. This command can be used to split a large file into several sequential smaller files for you to view, edit, or print out.

ct (user). Use `ct` to call a telephone number associated with a terminal line.

This command can be used to call a remote terminal and spawn a UNIX login prompt to that terminal. It can be issued to execute fairly tight control over remote login users.

cu (user). The `cu` command calls another UNIX System. It manages interactive messages and file transfers.

Use this command to become a user on another computer. The local UNIX computer you are dialing from becomes transparent to your session with the called computer.

cut (user). The `cut` command cuts out selected fields in an ASCII string of characters.

Use this command to extract text strings from a line of text when the whole line is unimportant to you. For example, if you wanted to use the day of the month to compute something or to make a decision, it would look like this:

```
#date | cut -c9-10
26
#
```

date (user). The `date` command prints the current date and time. Use it to "timestamp" your findings.

dd (user). Use `dd` to convert and copy files. It is especially good for moving files between different systems (UNIX and non-UNIX alike).

This is a very powerful command that not only facilitates transfer of files between systems but also provides a good measure of conversion options during transfer. For example, this command would be useful if you wanted to take a copy of many files off site and onto another UNIX system to audit.

df (admin). Use **df** to print the number of free blocks on one or more de-fined file systems.

When you need to know how much space is left in each file system, this command will tell you in blocks of 512 byte increments (or in kilobytes if you use a **-b** option). For example, typing in **df** would produce output like this:

```
/    (/dev/dsk/root    ):    33284 blocks    5351 files
/usr (/dev/dsk/usr     ):    56954 blocks    20696 files
```

diff, bdiff (user). This command compares two files (using **diff**) or two very large files (using **bdiff**), and prints out what must be changed to make them equal.

The **cmp** command described earlier also compares two files, but it dis-plays the location and number of characters that are different. That is, it an-swered the question, "Is there a difference?" This command answers the question, "What is different?" by displaying the differences from each of the compared files on a line-by-line basis. For example, if you wanted to com-pare two simple text files each containing a short sentence that differed by one character, and you typed **diff test_1 test_2**, the result would be something like this:

```
1c1
< This is a test file number 1.
- - - -
> This is a test file number 2.
#
```

On the other hand, if you typed in **#cmp test_1 test_2**, the result would be as follows:

```
test_1 test_2 differ: char 28, line 1
#
```

diffmk (user). The **diffmk** command marks the difference between two files using "change marks" in the margin for use with **nroff** or **troff** for-matters.

If your audit requires you to analyze the difference between the last few versions of a text document or several documents, this command would in-sert commands into a file for use by UNIX's **nroff** formatter that would cause change marks to be printed in the file's margin. The following is a typ-ical use:

```
#diffmk test_1 test_2 | nroff | lp
```

du (user). Use **du** to print out information about disk usage.

This is a very useful command to analyze disk usage. It, together with other commands, can quickly focus on potential problems or questionable parts of a file system you are investigating.

echo (user). The `echo` command sends messages or data to other users or into files. Use it to mimic keyboard entry in a batch file or to simulate interactive entry.

env (user). Use `env` to print the current settings of environmental variables.

There are hundreds of environmental settings that affect how certain commands work. To find out which settings are in effect, type in `env` at your terminal. The following is typical output:

```
HOME=/admin
MAIL=/usr/mail/sysadm
PATH=/sbin:/usr/sbin:/usr/bin
SHELL=/sbin/sh
TERM=/vt100
TZ=EST5EDT
```

file (user). The `file` command provides information about the type of file, based on the file's contents.

This command reads the contents of the specified file(s) and attempts to classify it as one of the following types:

- ASCII text
- English text
- Directory
- Empty
- Pure executable
- Commands test
- Symbolic link to ..
- [nt]roff, tbl, or eqn input text

For example, to classify all of the files in the current directory, you would type in **file** *. The result would look something like this:

```
Maint.fs    ascii text
test_1          ascii text
test_2          ascii text
x           [nt]roff, tbl, or eqn input text
```

find (user). The `find` command finds a named file by searching recursively from a starting directory.

Use this command when you know the file name you are looking for, but not where it is. It also works if you want to find a file by

- Permission
- Owner
- Group
- Link status
- Size
- Access time
- Modified time

For example, suppose you wanted to find where the **df** command was on a system. The command line and its results are as follows:

```
#find / -name df -print
/etc/df
/usr/bin/df
/usr/root.proto/etc/df
```

fuser (admin). Use `fuser` to see who is currently using a specific file or file structure.

This is a handy command to determine which processes are using a file. In an audit, for example, this command would be to set initial conditions before running a performance test.

grep (user). The `grep` command extracts and displays a line of text in a file based on a specified pattern. This command has 10 options, all of which are important.

Use this command to filter output from a test to isolate specific findings.

groups (user). The `groups` command displays members of specified groups. Use it to list the groups that can access the specified group's files. The following is an example of the command followed by its results

```
#groups bin
bin sys mail
#
```

head (user). The `head` command displays the first 10 lines of a text file.

This command is good for "peeking" at large text files. Use it to confirm the contents of an ASCII file without having to display or print the entire file.

kill (user). Use `kill` to terminate a process before it completes. Use this only to terminate processes that belong to you.

last (user). The `last` command prints out the last logins for specified or all users in reverse chronological order.

Use this command to audit who's been using the system in reverse chronological sequence. It answers the question, "When is the last time specified users logged into the system and for how long did they remain on?"

lpstat (user). The `lpstat` command provides line printer spooler status information. The `-t` option is useful to get the current state of all printers that the print scheduler knows about.

ls (user). Use `ls` to list the contents of a directory.

This command has 23 options, most of which you should know about. It is used extensively in creating different views for both auditing and benchmarking.

man (user). The `man` command displays entries from the reference manuals if they are stored online.

Use this command to produce the command's entry in the UNIX manual on your terminal. For example, if you wanted to learn all of the options of the `ls` command, you would type `man ls` and the complete manual pages for that command would be displayed at your terminal. Try it.

mkdir (user). Use `mkdir` to create new working directories to store audit or benchmark results.

more, page (user). The `more` and `page` commands display text information on a video terminal one page at a time.

When text from a file or process is directed at your terminal it will not stop until an end-of-file marker is encountered. Use `more` or `page` to gain control and view the displayed information one screenful at a time.

newgrp (user). The `newgrp` command logs you in as a member of a specified group. Use this command to audit group-specific access privileges.

nice (user). Use `nice` to run a command at a higher or lower priority.

You might consider running some of your audit processes at a lower priority so as to be less invasive or at a higher priority to be more preemptive.

nohup (user). Use nohup to run a command not affected by hangups and exits.

If your audit activities require you to remotely log in for certain examinations, you might want to leave a long process running and hang up your modem. Normally, UNIX will terminate your processes unless the nohup ("no hangup") option is specified.

od (user). Use od to dump file contents in any one of a number of formats.

Files containing special characters and binary files are not printable, but their contents can still be analyzed with od. At times this type of inspection will be the only way to unlock imponderable files that you need to know about.

pack (user). The pack command stores specified files in compressed form. Text files are reduced to about 65% to 70% of their original size.

You might need to inform users that they can gain 30% to 40% of disk space occupied by rarely used text files if they use this compression function.

pr (user). The pr command prints text files according to a specified format. It is typically used for pagination, spacing, and titling.

This command is particularly useful if you need to print out information that was piped to standard output.

ps (user). Use ps to display the processor's status.

This command gets you as close a "real time" view of the UNIX processor's status as you're going to get. The ps command has 12 options to help you better focus on information like the following:

- User's ID
- Process ID (unique number)
- Parent process ID
- When executed
- Elapsed execution time
- Processor utilization
- Process priority
- Memory address of process
- Process size in blocks
- Wait/sleep status

pwck, grpck (admin). Use pwck and grpck during the security audit to check the validity of passwords.

pwd (user). Use **pwd** to print the working directory's full pathname.

renice (user). Use **renice** to change the priority of a running process that you created.

rm,rmdir (user). Use **rm** or **rmdir** to remove any temporary files or directories you might have created.

sa1, sa2, sadc (admin). Use **sa1**, **sa2**, and **sadc** to access and run the system activity package to monitor system activities.

The **sa1** and **sa2** commands are actually shell scripts (batch command files) that control the executable program, **sadc**, which collects system data. The **sa1** and **sa2** commands cause data that is collected to be stored in directories read and reported on by **sar**, the UNIX activity report package.

Typically, **sa1** and **sa2** are entered into a text file for processing by **crontab**, which repeats the data collection at regularly specified intervals.

sar (user). Use **sar** to report system activity.

The activities of the system can be measured from different points of view:

- Inode searches per second (to determine efficiency of file access)
- Pathnames searches per second
- Reads per second
- Average number of disk transfers between the system and block devices
- Average accesses per second
- Read cache hit ratios
- Write cache hit ratio
- System calls per second
- Percent of device busy
- Average number of outstanding and serviced disk requests during time interval
- Data transfers per second
- Average number of milliseconds that a transfer request waits idly
- Average time in milliseconds to complete a transfer request
- Address translation page faults per second
- CPU usage (percent devoted to user, percent devoted to system, percent idle).

- Processes bound per second
- Processes reclaimed per second
- Process switches per second

script (user). The `script` command makes a typescript of a terminal session. That is, it records everything sent to a terminal and places it in a file.

Use this command to record an interactive terminal session. It's great for documenting your interactive audit sessions.

sleep (user). Use `sleep` to suspend execution for a specified number of seconds. If you need to separate events in a shell script (batch command file), `sleep` is the way to do it.

sort (user). Use `sort` to sort and/or merge files.

This command, along with its many options, is used to sort text files. More importantly, it sorts the text output of various processes.

strings (user). The `strings` command finds and displays the printable strings in an object file.

Use this command to inspect unknown object files to gain a clue as to what the software might be used for.

su (user). Use `su` to switch users or become the root user.

This command is used to take on another users permissions when logging on with the – option.

sum (user). The `sum` command prints the checksum and block count from a file.

Use this command to see if a binary file has changed or is different than a file saved previously.

sysadm (admin). Use `sysadm` to bypass many of the lower-level UNIX commands while auditing your system.

Invoke the computer manufacturer's administrative software. Many of the commands discussed in this section can be executed from menu-driven choices.

sysdef (admin). Use `sysdef` to display the system files used to build this UNIX system.

systemid (admin). Use `systemid` to display the system's manufacturer and the unique identification they have assigned to this computer.

tail (user). Use `tail` to display the last 10 lines of a text file.

This command is similar to the **head** command explained earlier. It is used to "peek" at the last lines of a text file.

tar (user). Use `tar` to save and restore multiple files on a single file archive.

This command is typically used to move files between different UNIX systems. It stores many files into a single file archive which can easily be moved between machines of different manufacturers with different word lengths and byte orientations.

tee (user). The `tee` command routes data to both the screen and a file at the same time.

Use this command to record your terminal session if the UNIX system you are auditing does not have a `script` command. The following example gives a **tee** command line and its output:

```
#ls −1 | tee saveit
total 58
-r--r--r--    1 root    5261 Aug 25 18:58 Maint.fs
-rw-rw-rw-    1 root     783 Aug 26 18:16 forkathy
#cat saveit
total 58
-r--r--r--    1 root    5261 Aug 25 18:58 Maint.fs
-rw-rw-rw-    1 root     783 Aug 26 18:16 forkathy
```

time, timex (user). The `time` or `timex` command prints the elapsed time it takes the system to execute any command typed from the command line.

Use this command to time a specific command or batch file run. The system will report real, user, and system time. With options, other measurements can be taken, such as the following:

- Fork/exec flag and system exit status
- Fraction of total available CPU time consumed by the process during its execution (total CPU time divided by elapsed time)
- Total Kcore minutes
- Mean core size
- CPU factor (user time divided by the sum of system time and user time)
- Total number of blocks read or written
- Total system activity during the length of this command

umask (user). The umask command determines the access permissions (modes) with which a file is created.

Use it to audit the file permissions that will be assigned to files created by a user.

uname (user). The uname command prints the current system name.

Use it to uniquely identify a system's name. With options, the following other system identification is available:

- nodename
- Operating system release
- Operating system version
- Machine's hardware name

uniq (user). The uniq command reports on repeated lines in a text file.

Use this command to report duplicate lines in a sorted text file. It will also report a count of the occurrences of each unique line.

uucheck (admin). Use uucheck to check UUCP directories and permissions file when auditing a system that uses UUCP communications facilities.

uustat (user). The uustat command is a UUCP status inquiry.

Use this command to report on all jobs in the UUCP queue. With options, the following information is available:

- Accessibility of all machines
- Job queues of all machines
- Remote status of all UUCP requests for specific systems
- Remote status of all UUCP requests for a specific user

vi, view (user). The vi and view commands invoke the primary UNIX editor for creating or updating text files.

Use view to access editor commands for searching and mobility without the possibility of modification. The visual editor (vi) is the primary UNIX editor. Although it has literally hundreds of commands (counting all of the possible combinations), you can get by learning 15 or 20 of them.

wc (user). Use wc for word, line, or character counts of text files, to count up findings from standard output.

who (user). Use who to see who is currently logged on to the system. This includes the user's terminal ID and the time login was initiated. Plenty of additional information is available with options:

- Process ID of user
- Time and date of last reboot
- System's "init" run level
- Last change to system clock
- Host names for remote users

whodo (admin). Use whodo to display who is doing what at the time the command is issued.

4

Audit Baseline

When you audit a system you will either want to reference an existing baseline or create one for future audits. The general-purpose nature of computers and their operating systems throws open all sorts of possibilities and permutations. If this is the first audit ever done on this system, you will need to establish a baseline reference. Once established, the baseline will be used as a reference for all inspections until it makes sense to incorporate new standards that redefine the baseline.

The systems' baseline answers the question, "How should the system be?" The baseline is driven by three primary factors:

- Resource administration files
- Application usage
- Production history

Detailed knowledge about these three factors enables you to reliably predict how this system should be at any time in the future.

The ideal time to document the baseline is when the system is first installed. The original system administrator and/or application designers had their reasons for choosing some resources and not choosing others, for extending or reducing the file system, for controlling local and remote access, for tuning the system to favor one kind of operation or another, and so on.

Creating a Baseline

If you don't already have a baseline, you need to create one. Let's say you've been using your system for some time and that you have both software and hardware support provided by the computer's manufacturer or some competent third party. To establish the baseline, you need to document starting conditions for the system's resource administration files, application usage, and production history.

Overview of the Creation Process

This section gives a brief overview of the baseline creation process.

Resource administration files

Follow these steps to document the starting conditions for the resource administration files:

1. Execute the procedure for a full system backup.
2. Do a complete UNIX installation from the original media or an exact copy of the original.
3. Create a "shadow" directory structure for all system resource files and tables.
4. Populate the shadow directory with copies of system resource files and tables.
5. Take a snapshot of disk usage and redirect the results into a text file at the root of the shadow directory.
6. Copy the populated shadow directory along with all of its subdirectories to removable magnetic media.
7. Restore the full production system saved in step 1.
8. Restore the shadow directory onto the production system.

Application usage

Application usage is nothing more than getting a handle on the intended use of the system. It means that you must get starting information about three things:

- Any non-UNIX software that is loaded
- Any data files that are being used, created, or extended
- The configuration of the system, including any network it may be a part of.

The system administrator should provide you with a list of other software that is loaded onto the UNIX system and available to users. This list should include both technical or system software products as well as end-user application products for things like office automation, accounting, or vertical market specialty products. These may be either purchased products or software developed by employees or contractors. Disk space used by these products can be measured by using the du -s on the full pathname of the product's root directory.

Major data file systems and/or database systems need to be defined in terms of both size and relationships that would allow growth predictions based on external measures understood and readily available to application users. As before, the size of these data sets can be measured using the du command.

The system administrator should be able to give you an exact hardware configuration of both the UNIX system you are auditing and its immediate network.

Production history

Finally, you must review all of the historical records that are available that involve the purchase, maintenance, application development, procedures, and system logs.

Details of baseline creation

This section defines exactly what you need to record as the starting point for the baseline, as well as how to record this information for use now and reuse in future audits.

System resource files

There are two kinds of system resource files:

- Those that record vital system parameters either incorporated directly into the UNIX kernel or used by UNIX programs to control what can or can't be done on this specific system.

- Those that record status or history information to help indicate what is or has been happening on this specific system.

By documenting the information in the resource files, you can monitor control of the system as a whole. You can also tell what has or has not changed between audits.

System resource files are defined by directory. You should find these files on any recent System V version of UNIX. The remainder of this section describes major directories that you might find on a typical UNIX system and the important system resource files they contain.

The root directory (/). This directory does not contain files that you need to deal with other than the names of other important directories to explore further. The root directory contains different subdirectories depending on the UNIX version and release you are auditing. The same subdirectories across recent UNIX versions and releases are likely to contain the same standard UNIX files and commands. System resource files are contained in the subdirectories from the root directory.

Remember that in UNIX, *root* is both the name of a real directory and a general concept. In either case it is used by the UNIX community as a starting point in a file system's hierarchy. When that hierarchy and the entire UNIX file system are the same, the directory is the root and it is named "root." When the hierarchy is not the entire UNIX file system but is some significant product or data set's file structure, it is considered the product's or data set's root directory. In this case, "root" is used in the conceptual sense.

/etc. The /etc directory is the focus of most of the files used by UNIX to control its resources. The primary user of this directory is the system administrator. It is owned by **root** and belongs to the **sys** group.

/etc/fstab. The **fstab** file is used to name the file system mount points that are configured for this UNIX machine.

When discussing file systems, it is important to distinguish between physical and logical file systems. UNIX permits a single *physical* file system (disk) to be partitioned as multiple *logical* file systems.

When UNIX is first booted, only the root file system is made available. At this point the UNIX system is running in single-user mode and/or at **init level 1**. When UNIX is brought to higher init levels (2,3, or 4), any file systems named in the **fstab** (file system table) are automatically attached. In later versions of release 3 and in release 4, remote file systems are also shown in this file.

Information in **fstab** answers two questions:

- What local (this machine) file systems are available at run level 2 and higher?

- What remote (other machines) file systems are available at run level 2 and higher?

The following is an example of the contents of **/etc/fstab**:

```
/dev/dsk/root      /            dg/ux rw d 0
/dev/dsk/swap      _area        swap sw x 0
/dev/dsk/usr       /usr         dg/ux rw d 0
```

/etc/group. The **group** file contains the names of groups and their respective members.

File access privileges are controlled by who owns the file and what group that individual belongs to. When a user is granted an account to log into a UNIX machine, he or she is assigned to a group. A user may belong to one or more groups. The access privileges to a UNIX file are *read*, *write* and *execute*. To read, write to, or execute (a program) file, a user needs to do one of the following:

- Access a file he or she owns
- Access a file owned by a group to which the user is assigned
- Access a file that has no group or user access restrictions

Information in the `group` file answers the following questions:

- What are the group names on this system?
- Which users belong to each group?

The following is an example of the contents of `/etc/group`:

```
root::0:root
other::1:
bin::2:root,bin,daemon
sys::3:root,bin,sys,adm
adm::4:root,adm,daemon
mail::5:mail,bin
lp::6:lp
uucp::8:uucp
daemon::12:root,daemon
operator::18:adm
nfs::38:nfs
ftp::39:ftp
general::100:
+
```

/etc/gettydefs. The `gettydefs` file contains available terminal settings and characteristics that can be assigned to communication ports.

Because the UNIX operating system is an open system, it can be accessed from or have access to literally hundreds of different serial devices (such as terminals, modems, and printers). The `gettydefs` file makes it possible to define the characteristics of most of the existing serial devices in the market.

The characteristics of a device are assigned to the port it connects to by choosing an entry, identified by a label in the `gettydefs` file, and including that label in the port's record in another file called `inittab` (described next).

Information from the `gettydefs` file answers the following questions:

- What are the serial device characteristics supported by this system?
- What are the alternative speeds and settings that will be attempted when a user logs into a port?

The following is an example of the contents of `/etc/gettydefs`:

```
console# B9600 ECHO ECHOE ECHOK KILL ^u ERASE ^? INTR ^c HUPCL CS8
OPOST ONLCR ICRNL CREAD CLOCAL ISTRIP # B9600 ECHO ECHOE ECHOK IEX-
TEN KILL ^u ERASE ^? INTR ^c ICANON CS8 OPOST ISTRIP CREAD CLOCAL
IXON IXOFF ISIG ICRNL ONLCR TAB3 #login: #console


9600# B9600 ECHO ECHOE ECHOK KILL ^u ERASE ^? INTR ^c HUPCL CS8
OPOST ONLCR ICRNL CREAD CLOCAL ISTRIP # B9600 ECHO ECHOE ECHOK IEX-
TEN KILL ^u ERASE ^? INTR ^c ICANON CS8 OPOST ISTRIP CREAD CLOCAL
IXON IXOFF ISIG ICRNL ONLCR TAB3 #login: #9600


9600EP# B9600 ECHO ECHOE ECHOK KILL ^u ERASE ^? INTR ^c HUPCL
PARENB CS7 OPOST ONLCR ICRNL CREAD CLOCAL # B9600 ECHO ECHOE ECHOK
IEXTEN KILL ^u ERASE ^? INTR ^c ICANON PARENB CS7 OPOST ISTRIP
CREAD CLOCAL IXON IXOFF ISIG ICRNL ONLCR TAB3 #login: #9600EP


19200# B19200 ECHO ECHOE ECHOK KILL ^u ERASE ^? INTR ^c HUPCL CS8
OPOST ONLCR ICRNL CREAD CLOCAL # B19200 ECHO ECHOE ECHOK IEXTEN
KILL ^u ERASE ^? INTR ^c ICANON CS8 OPOST ISTRIP CREAD CLOCAL IXON
IXOFF ISIG ICRNL ONLCR TAB3 #login: #19200


19200EP# B19200 ECHO ECHOE ECHOK KILL ^u ERASE ^? INTR ^c HUPCL
PARENB CS7 OPOST ONLCR ICRNL CREAD CLOCAL # B19200 ECHO ECHOE ECHOK
IEXTEN KILL ^u ERASE ^? INTR ^c ICANON PARENB CS7 OPOST ISTRIP
CREAD CLOCAL IXON IXOFF ISIG ICRNL ONLCR TAB3 #login: #19200EP


M1200# B1200 ECHO ECHOE ECHOK KILL ^u ERASE ^? INTR ^c HUPCL CS8
OPOST ONLCR ICRNL CREAD ISTRIP # B1200 ECHO ECHOE ECHOK IEXTEN KILL
^u ERASE ^? INTR ^c HUPCL ICANON CS8 OPOST ICRNL ONLCR ISTRIP CREAD
IXON IXOFF ISIG TAB3 #login: #M1200


M2400# B2400 ECHO ECHOE ECHOK KILL ^u ERASE ^? INTR ^c HUPCL CS8
OPOST ONLCR ICRNL CREAD ISTRIP # B2400 ECHO ECHOE ECHOK IEXTEN KILL
^u ERASE ^? INTR ^c HUPCL ICANON CS8 OPOST ICRNL ONLCR ISTRIP CREAD
IXON IXOFF ISIG TAB3 #login: #M2400


M4800# B4800 ECHO ECHOE ECHOK KILL ^u ERASE ^? INTR ^c HUPCL CS8
OPOST ONLCR ICRNL CREAD ISTRIP # B4800 ECHO ECHOE ECHOK IEXTEN KILL
^u ERASE ^? INTR ^c HUPCL ICANON CS8 OPOST ICRNL ONLCR ISTRIP CREAD
IXON IXOFF ISIG TAB3 #login: #M4800
```

```
M9600# B9600 ECHO ECHOE ECHOK KILL ^u ERASE ^? INTR ^c HUPCL CS8
OPOST ONLCR ICRNL CREAD ISTRIP # B9600 ECHO ECHOE ECHOK IEXTEN KILL
^u ERASE ^? INTR ^c HUPCL ICANON CS8 OPOST ICRNL ONLCR ISTRIP CREAD
IXON IXOFF ISIG TAB3 #login: #M9600


M300# B300 ECHO ECHOE ECHOK KILL ^u ERASE ^? INTR ^c HUPCL CS8
OPOST ONLCR ICRNL CREAD ISTRIP # B300 ECHO ECHOE ECHOK IEXTEN KILL
^u ERASE ^? INTR ^c HUPCL ICANON CS8 OPOST ICRNL ONLCR ISTRIP CREAD
IXON IXOFF ISIG TAB3 #login: #M300
```

/etc/inittab. The `inittab` file specifies what UNIX is to do after its initial startup (boot).

You might want UNIX to stop at the administrative level (init level 1) instead of going right to multiuser mode (init level 2 or 3). At the administrative level, all file systems are mounted and available to the system administrator and no one else. Besides controlling the way the system is brought up to full strength, `inittab` specifies how to treat each serial port (tty) if and when a login is requested.

The information in `inittab` answers the following questions:

- What programs will be executed automatically at each run level?
- What processes run continuously within each run level?
- What serial device characteristics are assigned to each port? (See the discussion of `gettydefs`.)

The following is an example of the contents of `/etc/inittab`:

```
#
def:s:initdefault:
fsc::bootwait:/sbin/chk.fsck                    </dev/console
>/dev/console 2>&1
dat::bootwait:/usr/sbin/init.d/chk.date         </dev/console
>/dev/console 2>&1
set::bootwait:/usr/sbin/init.d/chk.system       </dev/console
>/dev/console
>/dev/console 2>&1
set::bootwait:/usr/sbin/init.d/chk.system       </dev/console
>/dev/console 2>&1
dev::bootwait:/usr/sbin/init.d/chk.devlink      </dev/console
>/dev/console 2>&1
#
rc0:0:wait:/sbin/rc.init 0 >/dev/console 2>&1
rc1:1:wait:/sbin/rc.init 1 >/dev/console 2>&1
rc2:2:wait:/sbin/rc.init 2 >/dev/console 2>&1
rc3:3:wait:/sbin/rc.init 3 >/dev/console 2>&1
```

```
rc4:4:wait:/sbin/rc.init 4 >/dev/console 2>&1
rc5:5:wait:/sbin/rc.init 5 >/dev/console 2>&1
rc6:6:wait:/sbin/rc.init 6 >/dev/console 2>&1
#
# the getty is more secure than su since su is always on
console
con::respawn:/usr/sbin/getty console console
sec::off:#/sbin/su — 1 </dev/console >/dev/console 2>&1
#
01:234:respawn:/etc/getty tty01 9600 vt100 #Standard TTY
```

/etc/passwd. The `passwd` file contains user information for anyone who has been granted an account to log into this system. Each user has an entry in this file consisting of a number of fields separated by colons. The entry is terminated by a new line.

The information in this file answers the following questions:

- How many user accounts are maintained on this system?
- How strict is security enforced on this system?
- What are the names of each account and to whom do they belong?
- Are there any accounts with no password?
- What is each account's home (starting) directory?
- What command interpreter (shell) is in effect immediately after logging in?

The following is an example of the contents of `/etc/inittab`:

```
root::0:1:  Special Admin login:/:/sbin/sh
sysadm::0:0: Regular Admin login:/admin:/sbin/sh
daemon:*:1:1: Daemon Login for daemons needing perms:/:/sbin/sh
bin:*:2:2:  Admin :/bin:
sys:*:3:3:  Admin :/usr/src:
adm:*:4:4:   Admin :/usr/adm:/sbin/sh
uucp:*:5:5:  UUCP Login:/usr/spool/uucp:/usr/lib/uucp/uucico
nuucp:*:5:1: UUCP Admin Login :/usr/lib/uucp:/sbin/sh
lp:*:6:2:   Printer:/usr/lib:/sbin/sh
mail:*:8:1:  Sendmail Login for mail
delivery:/usr/mail:/usr/bin/mail
sync::19:1:  Disk Update Login without password:/:/bin/sync
yp:*:37:37:  YP Admin :/usr/etc/yp:/sbin/sh
nfs:*:38:38: NFS Admin :/:/sbin/sh
ftp:*:39:39: FTP guest Login:/var/ftp:/sbin/sh
nobody:*:65534:65534::/:
+:
```

/etc/profile. The `profile` file contains the default user initialization commands or settings that are executed once a user's login is acceptable and before any other requests are accepted from that user.

Certain global options are in force by default for the entire user community. This file eliminates the need to repeat these options for each individual user. Global settings addressed by `profile` include the following:

- Timezone
- Default terminal type
- Paths to search for commands
- File creation mask that sets access privileges on files that are created

The information in this file answers the question, "What is the new account user's operating environment like?"

The following is an example of the contents of `/etc/profile`:

```
#
# The profile that all logins get before .profile
trap "" 2 3
#       Set LOGNAME
export LOGNAME
#       Set TZ.
if [ -f /etc/TIMEZONE ]
then
.       /etc/TIMEZONE
elif [ -f /etc/TIMEZONE.proto ]
then
.       /etc/TIMEZONE.proto
fi
#       Set TERM.
if      [ -z "$TERM" ]
then
        TERM=vt100  # for standard async terminal
        export TERM
fi
# Login and -su shells get /etc/profile services.
# -rsh is given its environment in its .profile.
case "$0" in
-su )
        export PATH
        ;;
-sh )
        export PATH
        # Allow the user to break the M-O-T-D only.
        trap "trap " 2" 2
```

```
    if [ -f /usr/bin/cat ] ; then
            cat -s /etc/motd
    fi
    trap "" 2
    if [ -f /usr/bin/mail ] ; then
            if mail -e ; then
                    echo "you have mail"
            fi
    fi
    ;;
esac
#    set the umask for more secure operation
#umask 022
trap 2 3
```

These default user settings may be customized for each user by a "hidden file" in each user's *home directory* (the user's starting directory at login time) called `.profile` (commonly called "dot profile").

/dev. The `dev` directory contains special files called device nodes.

UNIX treats input and output to connected hardware the same way it treats input and output to any logical file. That is, it insulates the application software from having to interact differently based on the specific characteristics of each different hardware device.

A listing of the files in this directory (using `ls`) will tell the auditor what nodes have been defined to the system, and what is available for use or assignment.

/var. The `var` directory contains all of the subdirectories and files that grow and diminish dynamically as the system is used. Hence, *var* implies *variable*. In older UNIX systems, the subdirectories listed here were subdirectories of `/usr` instead of `/var`. During these years of transition, compatibility is gracefully handled by linking `/usr/subdirectory` to `/var/subdirectory`.

The resource files in this directory usually indicate the system's current status or record important historical information. Typical UNIX subdirectories that are distributed under `/var` are described in the following paragraphs.

/var/adm. The `adm` subdirectory contains data that was collected by the systems accounting package. The accounting package is a primary tool for the UNIX auditor. When activated, it collects data at the transaction level (such as logins, logouts, date changes, and reboots). It documents hardware resource allocation for each login transaction by tracking CPU, memory, and disk access data. The resource information stored in these files answers hundreds of questions about performance and usage.

You needn't be concerned with the files in this directory because you can get at the information they contain in an orderly and straightforward manner by running the system accounting reports described in chapter 7.

/var/Build. Not all UNIX software suppliers will call this subdirectory *Build*. Some will call it *system*. Regardless of what it is called, it is usually empty at the time of initial distribution because it serves as a "work area" for rebuilding the UNIX kernel. From time to time, the system's administrator might want to *tune* the operating system (change how it allocates its resources). These changes must be built into the UNIX kernel before they can become effective.

This directory is a perfect illustration of the "variable" concept of the /var directory. When used, Build goes from being empty, to containing files that occupy between one and two megabytes, to being left empty again within the span of 30 minutes.

/var/mail. UNIX mail for all users is stored in mail. There will be a subdirectory for each user containing mail that is to be delivered, retained, or redirected.

/var/news. News from other network systems or from this system is stored in subdirectories of news on a dynamic basis. This subdirectory's value should be questioned and its resource utilization needs measured. In general, more academic systems tend to support news subdirectories. On commercial and scientific systems, these subdirectories tend to be a waste of space and computing resources.

/var/opt. Application packages are usually stored in opt. That is, the main or *root* directories of purchased or developed systems are usually attached here. If other software is not stored here, find out why not. If non-UNIX software is arbitrarily loaded in different directories and in different file systems, you should recommend that it be consolidated here. If there are good reasons to physically locate the software elsewhere, consider linking it in this directory.

/var/spool. UNIX uses spoolers for shared devices and facilities such as the line printer (LP) and machine-to-machine communications (UUCP). Files waiting their turn for printing or remote transmission reside in spool. This too, is a good example of the variable nature of /var.

/var/preserve. Text editors save copies of current editing sessions in order to be able to restore a user's file if it is abruptly terminated. For example, if a user shuts off the video terminal before saving the file that was just created, there is a good chance of restoring most of that file from the preserve directory.

/usr. The usr subdirectory contains files (commands, programs, and data) and subdirectories accessible to most users. In older UNIX systems, administrators were encouraged to mount or add a "user account" subdirectory in /usr. Newer UNIX Versions provide a subdirectory off of root, /home, for that purpose.

/usr/admin. Most UNIX suppliers today provide administrative packages (or *admin shells*) to help system administrators maintain systems entrusted to their care without requiring that they be UNIX system programmers. These facilities are generally friendly and easy to use.

Programs, help files and lookup data required by these packages are stored in /usr/admin.

/usr/bin. All users have access to the UNIX commands in bin.

/usr/catman. UNIX documentation is available online because the text is stored in subdirectories below /usr/catman.

/usr/etc. The /usr/etc directory contains important resource definition and configuration files.

/usr/etc/termcap. The termcap file contains all of the possible video-terminal dependent characteristics supported by this system. Each user is assigned a terminal type (such as vt100 or D215). This assignment is used by UNIX software to fetch the terminal's characteristics from termcap.

If a user is assigned a terminal type that does not match the terminal he or she is using, the interactive session will get out of control once terminal-dependent software is invoked.

/usr/master.d/*. Files contained in the /usr/master.d directory describe the rules of configuration for the UNIX system. The manufacturer may use any number of names for these files that incorporate the manufacturer's company or product name. The following information is found here:

- Naming conventions
- Device configuration rules and dependencies
- Input feeds to the kernel configuration program
- Supported network protocols
- Keyword translations and default values
- Default values of tunable parameters

/usr/include. The include files are those required by system software.

/usr/lib. The /usr/lib subdirectory contains library files required by such functions as system accounting, font management, manufacturer specific hardware, help data files, mail, spell checkers, formatters, UUCP, UNIX software development packages, and terminal information.

/usr/local. The `/usr/local` subdirectory contains site-specific files. This directory is empty unless the system administrator adds files here.

/usr/release. Release information for this release as well as any past "minor" releases will be stored in `/release`. These are text files provided by the manufacturer that describe what is added, deleted, and fixed from one release to another.

/usr/opt. Optional UNIX packages provided by the UNIX supplier are stored in `/opt`.

/usr/sbin. Commands for system administrators only are stored in `sbin`.

/usr/src. If your site has UNIX source code, it is stored in `/src`.

/usr/stand. Standalone programs and boot utilities are stored in `stand`.

Recording information

In order to examine all of the file systems, you must record the pertinent details of hundreds of directories and subdirectories. One way to do this is to attach a *shadow directory structure* somewhere in the UNIX file system and populate it with pertinent information about the files in each of the system's directories.

Copy two kinds of information into this shadow directory:

- Exact copies of certain resource files
- Information about files in all directories

Creating the "shadow."   A good name for the shadow directory is *baseline*. It should hold the relative position of the root directory in the real system. Make the directory at any convenient place that is **not** part of the UNIX distribution file system. One good place for `baseline` is in the parent directory for user accounts (either `home` or, in older UNIX systems, `usr`). Alternatively, you can create a shadow directory under `/opt`, as shown in Figure 4.1.

Let's go ahead and create `baseline` under `/home` by typing the following:

```
cd /home
mkdir baseline
cd baseline
pwd
```

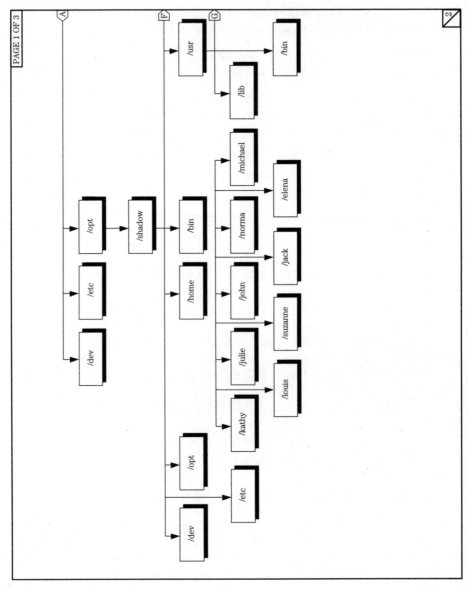

Figure 4.1   A shadow directory attached to the main directory.

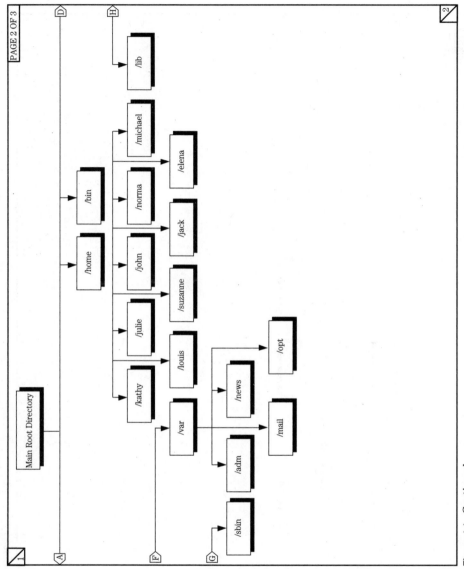

Figure 4.1 *Continued.*

Figure 4.1 *Continued.*

```
/home/baseline
```

At this point it would be wise to get the system's administrator to create an auditor's login account with the home directory `/home/baseline`. To log in to that auditor's account, type the following:

```
login: auditor
password: your password
```

To be certain that the administrator has defined your home account correctly, type the following:

```
pwd
/home/baseline
```

Chapter 6 describes programs included in this book that actually create and populate the shadow directory. You could also create the appropriate directories manually. The following example shows how to create the shadow structure manually for a small UNIX system:

```
mkdir etc dev var/adm var/Build var/mail
\var/news var/opt var/spool var/preserve
#
mkdir usr/admin usr/bin usr/catman usr/etc
\ usr/master.d usr/include usr/lib usr/local
\usr/release usr/opt usr/sbin usr/src usr/stand
#
```

You could then verify that what you've created is correct by issuing a disk usage command with a detail option:

```
du -a
```

The response from **du -a** printed to your screen should be something like this:

```
0    ./etc
0    ./dev
0    ./var/adm
0    ./var/Build
0    ./var/mail
0    ./var/news
0    ./var/opt
0    ./var/spool
0    ./var/preserve
1    ./var
0    ./usr/admin
```

```
0     ./usr/bin
0     ./usr/catman
0     ./usr/etc
0     ./usr/etc/master.d
0     ./usr/include
0     ./usr/lib
0     ./usr/local
0     ./usr/release
0     ./usr/opt
0     ./usr/sbin
0     ./usr/src
0     ./usr/stand
1     ./usr
3     .
(EOF)
```

You have now created the shadow directory structure. You can use or modify this example to suit your system's UNIX distribution, which might not agree with the structure shown above. Be certain to include directories even if they are empty. The idea is to get a baseline "snapshot" of the system at some point in time.

This book contains *shell scripts* (programs) that you can use to do this process automatically and much more thoroughly. These are discussed in chapter 6.

Populating the shadow directory. The current system information that makes up the baseline view must be copied and/or created. That is, certain resource files must be copied from the production system into their baseline directory structure, or information about certain files and/or directories must be stored in their respective baseline directories for comparison later.

Before actually populating the shadow directory, let's create a shortcut to specify /home/baseline so you won't need to type it out each time you need to refer to it:

```
b='pwd';export b
echo $b
/home/baseline
```

Copy files as follows:

```
cd /etc
cp fstab group gettydefs inittab passwd profile $b/etc
cd /usr/etc
cp termcap $b/usr/etc
cp master.d/* $b/usr/etc/master.d
cd
```

The next step is to gather and record baseline information about all of the directories to be examined. The basic process is to gather information about all directories and files and place it into *README* files in their respective shadow directory. The plan is to keep the README files in a strict predefined format so you can use UNIX commands to create them and make automated comparisons with future production systems.

To create README files, first copy the shell scripts provided with this book into the /home/baseline directory and be certain that /home/base line is in your $PATH. To see if it is, type this:

```
echo $PATH
```

The system should respond by displaying all directories that will be searched for any commands you issue, for example:

```
/sbin:/usr/sbin:/usr/bin:/home/baseline
```

If /home/baseline was not in your path you could set it as follows:

```
PATH=$PATH:/home/baseline; export PATH
```

Then, run the batch version of the baseline recording script, capture. (See a printout of the contents in appendix A.) The detailed procedure to do this is described in chapter 6.

The capture script creates one "master" README file in the baseline's root directory that provides global system information to the UNIX Auditor. The contents of this file provides the following information:

- The name given to this specific audit and the time and date the data was collected
- The full pathname of the root directory being examined
- The full pathname of the baseline's root directory (the start of the shadow directory)
- The total number of directories being examined
- The UNIX kernel file name along with the version, release, and node name of the system
- The specific hardware on which the kernel was intended to run
- Free space currently available on this system
- Total blocks (excluding swap space) currently in use

The capture program creates a README file for each directory it analyzes and places that README file into the examined directory's shadow directory. Figure 4.2 compares the root directory structure with the shadow directory structure.

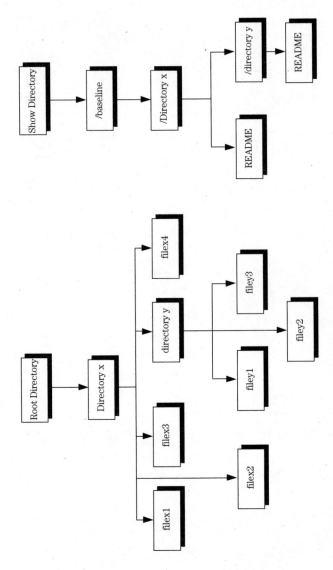

Figure 4.2 A root file structure compared to its shadow file structure.

The contents of a README file provides the following information about each examined directory:

- The name given to this specific audit and the time and date the data was collected.
- Full directory name that was examined
- Name of the directory's owner
- Number of directory files in the examined directory
- Number of linked files in the examined directory
- Number of executable files in the examined directory
- Number of "other" files in the examined directory
- Total character count for all files in this directory
- Details of each file in this directory
- A 16-bit *checksum value* of the contents of every file in the directory, such as the following:
  —Permissions
  —Owner
  —Group
  —Size in characters
  —Date of last modification (or creation)
  —Name of file
  —Checksum (16 bits) of contents
  —Estimate of file type based on its contents

Your operating system distribution baseline is now complete. Baseline information for a newly installed system takes very little room on disk. The disk usage on the Aviion used to write this book was 1156 blocks of baseline files for 103,602 total blocks used, which is 1.1 percent of the disk space.

Application Usage

Application usage involves programs and data running on a specific hardware or network equipment configuration.

Software

Applications justify computer ownership, and for the majority of systems are the most important aspect. Applications can consist of one or more of the following in any combination:

- Purchased application software products
- Custom-developed application software

- Purchased file management software (RDBMSs)
- Purchased software development tools (such as CASE tools, application generators, and specialized 4GL tools)
- Purchased communications software
- UNIX productivity extensions and compilers
- Custom-developed utilities and automated procedures

Data

Along with software come the data files that are created, updated, and referenced. Another dimension about data needs to be recorded if the data set consists of related records that grow in response to known transactions. Transaction-based systems need to be carefully monitored for unpredicted growth, purge effectiveness, and capacity management.

Configuration information

Hardware certainly is a major factor influencing software performance. Performance expectations, in particular, are set and reviewed based on the specifics of the hardware on which the software is running. If the hardware configuration or the network's topology is not readily available, use one or more of the following sources to create it:

- Equipment purchase documents
- Equipment maintenance agreements
- Interviews (of department or office managers)
- A physical inventory

Recording information

All of the different kinds of software should be organized into different directory structures according to their installation instructions or the judgment of the system administrator (e.g., attached to `/var/option`). Once in place, directories should be added to the shadow structure, baseline, and an interactive recording should be taken using the `capture` shell script provided with this book—or the `capture` script can be used on the entire file system.

Data directory structures also need to be identified to the baseline and `capture` needs to be used to create the respective README files for each directory.

Appendix 2 shows a relational model for predicting and monitoring actual data growth versus expected growth for transaction-oriented systems. Prerequisites to creating such models are knowledge of the internal structures of the database. When using purchased software packages, be certain to interview the package supplier to obtain this information.

Configuration information must be recorded and maintained with each baseline version.

Production History

Production history should be kept and made available in two forms. First, the raw output of any significant event on the system should be logged. Second, an interpreted view of one or more logged events, including experience-based responses to the events, should be logged. This second form of system history is normally kept in a *procedure book* organized by topic.

System logs

Production systems, like ships at sea, have logs to report on production events, errors, and external events that affect system operations. These events should be reported in sequential order with as much detail as possible. There are basic UNIX files like `/etc/wtmp` that contain information about past operations. There are sets of files that are a result of activating UNIX accounting that provide detailed information to help you get an accurate profile of production usage (discussed in detail in chapter 7). Then there are logging systems supplied by different manufacturers, that chronicle console errors and/or hardware diagnostic errors. As of this writing, there are no standards defined for these types of logs. It is here that manufacturers have the opportunity to "add value" to their products.

Procedures

Procedure books should be compiled from the moment the system gets ready to go into production. Most UNIX systems come with several thousands of pages of documentation. For any specific system, the administrator only needs a fraction of that to handle any and all situations.

Procedure books are written to be a summary of knowledge and experience customized to a particular site. Procedures are driven more by application usage than by UNIX or technical issues.

Recording information

System logs are recorded primarily on an automated basis by the system accounting package or by a manufacturer's logging feature. For older versions of UNIX, administrators sometimes leave a small printer attached in parallel with a console terminal so that all console messages are immediately available on hard copy.

Site procedures, on the other hand, should be extracted from time to time on an ongoing basis from the system logs and the collective experience gained from daily operations. They should be written up and organized.

Saving the Baseline

The baseline recordings need to be saved in three ways:

- Full system save
- Baseline information only (magnetic media, two copies)
- Baseline information only (hard copy printout)

The baseline information should be kept with the remainder of the audit results in a safe and secure place, preferably off-site.

After establishing the baseline, an audit can be conducted that measures the current system with a reasonable reference to the past. Using baseline information you can examine and report on both current system status and the changes to the system since the last audit.

The files that are examined by the `capture` script should never include a previously captured shadow directory structure. For that reason it is important that you remove all baseline files at the end of the audit or at least before `capture` is run for the next audit.

5

Audit Previews

The previous chapters set up the basic ideas and concepts required to conduct the UNIX audit. This chapter, and the next three, discuss the actual examinations that should be carried out in a full audit. A number of activities that must be handled prior to actually examining UNIX itself, alluded to in the first chapter of this book, are addressed here.

The Management Meeting

Your mission to audit an important control system for a corporation needs to come from a fairly high level of executive management. In fact, be suspicious if this is not the case. There is a thin line between *auditing* and *breaking and entering*. Once you're assured that your "search warrant" is official, schedule a meeting with the management team most affected by your audit activities.

If the company is small or if the system you are auditing is strictly a departmental one, the management team should consist of the following:

- President or department head
- Key employee for accounting or administration
- System administrator

If the company and the system you are auditing are large, the management team at the meeting should include executives in charge of the following departments:

- MIS
- Finance
- Administration
- Major user departments

The goal of your meeting is to gain consensus and support for your mission. You will want everyone's cooperation to get the kind of information you need in a timely manner. To obtain your goal, the meeting must accomplish the following objectives:

1. Inform all key players about your audit.
2. Set expectations for both resource use and benefit.
3. Briefly describe the methods you will use.
4. Give examples of typical findings and recommendations.
5. Hand out a schedule of events.
6. Hand out a list of the documentation that you will require. Get the commitment of responsible parties to get each item on the list to you.
7. Ask about application usage and volume.
8. Ask about any specific information anyone might hope to gain from your audit.
9. Ask for their help.

User Interviews

While you are waiting for the right documentation to be gathered, you can conduct user interviews. It is helpful to classify users broadly by type of use: application users, technical users, and system users.

Application users do not require any system knowledge to do their work. These users do require the application skills necessary to use industry-specific software or office automation products. Technical users do require some system knowledge depending on their technical role. The technical user uses the system in totally different ways than application users. System and database administrators are system users, and are the most important individuals to interview.

Application users

Find out from the head of the application user departments who their key users are. If there are many kinds of users, ask for one typical user from each group. Your interviews with these users can be brief and relatively un-structured. Be sure to cover the following topics:

Usage.   What do you use the computer for? How many hours per day do you use the system? How many other users use the system in the same or a similar manner? Can you describe average start and end times for certain activities? Daily? Weekly? Monthly? Are there cyclical or event-driven intense uses of the system? Have there been any changes since the last audit?

Security.   What are the security habits among users? How frequently are passwords changed? Do users log out when they leave their terminals? Do users have remote access capabilities? If so, what are the access procedures? What are exit procedures on termination or resignation? Do you have or know of passwords other than your own? Is your password easy to remember? Is your password a name, a word found in the dictionary, a numeric ID that can easily be associated with you? Have there been any changes from the last audit?

Reliability.   How available is your system? How frequently has it been "down?" Does it behave inconsistently? Have there been any changes since the last audit?

Functionality.   How does your application software work? What do you like and dislike about it? Is it easy to use? Does it always work the same way? Do old bugs reappear after they've been fixed? Have there been any changes since the last audit?

Integrity.   Does your input always "take?" Do you get excessive lock messages? Have you ever had to reenter your work? If so, please describe. Have there been any changes since the last audit?

Performance.   How responsive are your interactive sessions? Are some times better than others? Please describe. Do long reports slow down the response time? Have there been any changes since the last audit?

Service.   What is the procedure that you follow to report on problems? To request services or enhancements? Are your requests acknowledged and serviced in a timely manner? Explain.

Ideal system.   Can you describe the ideal system to work on? What system features or qualities are most and least important to you? Can you quantify the impact of these ideal features or describe the impact they would have on your work?

Technical users

The technical staff consists of program development and maintenance personnel. These users are comfortable with technology and are inclined to optimize their working environments. While this should be expected and encouraged, it needs to be examined to ensure the "optimizations" are not at the expense of other users' reasonable expectations.

Ideally the technical staff should be isolated from the production system on their own equipment. Technical users provide a unique and helpful insight to an auditor. Listening to their comments and reviewing measurements they might have taken to document their claims can help you focus your audit on troublesome areas or targets of opportunity.

The technical users' interview should cover the same points described for application users plus the following:

Tools. How do you develop or maintain software? What compilers or UNIX utilities are you using? What third-party development products are you using? How are new updates and releases of tools installed? Have you read all of the release notes supplied with the current operating system and all of the development products you are using? Have there been changes from the last audit?

Reliability. Do you know if any of the products you use are flawed? Have the manufacturers or product user groups provided you with problem or bug lists? Have you identified the problems you need to build "workarounds" for? How about the software you have developed? Is there a backlog of reported problems that you haven't gotten to yet? Do you have any tracking system or records management facility to report on all application problems? Have there been changes from the last audit?

Performance. What is your opinion about the system's performance? Developing applications? User's point of view? Have there been changes from the last audit?

System users

In smaller companies, the system administrator is responsible for the well-being of the entire installation. For larger companies, the system administrator's role might be focused on UNIX administration alone. Regardless of the size of the company, however, the system administrator must have comprehensive knowledge of all system activities and related events in order to carry out his or her mission. For this reason, the system administrator should be your constant companion.

At larger installations, similar kinds of responsibilities are borne by database administrators. This type of system user is essentially responsible for third-party data management affecting storage, performance, and overall data integrity. This individual is usually a database specialist with advanced knowledge of the operating system.

The most useful and accurate insights about how UNIX is used and performing should come from these individuals.

The system users' interview should cover the same points described for application users plus the following:

History. What stage of the system lifecycle are you in? Do you have sufficient resources? What do you need and why? Can you discuss the evolution of the system since the last audit or from installation? What, if any, resource changes are being considered, proposed, or scheduled?

Day to day. What are your regular procedures? Automated? Manual? What are your event-driven and emergency procedures? Who fulfills your responsibilities when you are absent? How do you manage records of system events and service requests? Have there been any changes from the last audit?

Support. How would you rate the support you get for hardware? The operating system? From third-party software suppliers? From in-house development or maintenance staff? Have there been changes from the last audit?

Document Review

Reviewing system related documents is as important as any UNIX system measurement. System documents give your technical examinations context. They define intentions, expectations, and motive that can never be learned using UNIX tools alone. The documents you need to review are the original purchase and installation documents, and the subsequent documents that have been created since the system was released to production.

Original purchase and installation

The original documents that you need to examine include the following:

- Request for proposal (RFP)
- Vendor proposal
- Purchase and implementation contract
- Purchase order(s)
- Vendor invoice, proof of delivery, installation, and payment
- Original maintenance agreements
- Product registration and warranty documents
- Software licenses
- Proof of replacement insurance

Organize these documents into a separate, companion deliverable called *Audited System Documents*.

Typical questions that should be answered by these documents include the following:

- Requests for proposals
  —Why did the company buy the computer?
  —What was the computer supposed to be used for?
  —What alternatives, if any, were acceptable?
  —What was the priority of each requirement?
  —What other systems did this system need to interface with?
  —On what criteria was vendor selection made?
  —What were the estimated volumes and type of usage?
  —What was the expected growth rate of usage, functionality, and storage?
  —What were the expected staffing requirements for operating the purchased equipment?
  —What were the expected training and support requirements?

- Vendor Proposal
  —What was the vendor's response to the request for proposal before contract negotiation?
  —Was the vendor's response well mapped to each requirement in the RFP?
  —What specific products and services was the vendor proposing to sell?
  —How much responsibility did the vendor agree to accept for all of the proposed products and services and especially for resold or subcontracted items?
  —What were the proposed terms and conditions?
  —Were the vendor's prices competitive?
  —Were there specific added-value items that were to be included at no extra charge?

- Implementation contract
  —What were the results of negotiation?
  —What was the specific list of deliverables?
  —What was each party responsible for?
  —What were the delivery and payment schedules?
  —What were the warranty obligations?
  —What, if any, were the restrictive covenants (confidentiality, solicitation, competitive restrictions)?
  —What were the acceptance criteria?
  —What were the limits of liability?

- Purchase order(s)
  —What was actually purchased?

—Was the purchase order conditional?
—When were items ordered?
—Who authorized the purchase order?

- Proof of delivery or installation
  —What was actually charged?
  —When were the goods and services delivered?
  —When were products first installed and available for use?
  —Were goods and services ever paid for? When?

- Original maintenance agreements
  —What coverage was provided for in the maintenance agreement? How many days and hours were covered?
  —What were the effective dates of the coverage? Was the starting date dependent on some other date or event?
  —How were the coverage effective dates coordinated with the end of the warranty periods?
  —What are the obligations of each party?
  —What are the limits of liability of this agreement? Is a service escalation policy defined?

- Product registration and warranty
  —Is there proof that all product registration documents were filled out and sent?
  —Are there confirming notices that warranty coverage has commenced?
  —Has failure to register jeopardized the product's warranty?

- Software licenses
  —Does each software product have its own license granting rights to use for an agreed-upon term?
  —Have the license registrations been confirmed with the original product authors?
  —Are you in possession of original, serialized distribution media?

- Proof of replacement insurance
  —Is the equipment, software, and related support products adequately covered by insurance?
  —Do you have umbrella coverage for valuable papers?

Subsequent documentation

Once the system is released into production, other pertinent documentation is created relating to the systems normal maintenance, growth, problems. These include the following:

- Maintenance agreement renewals
- New-purchase related documents

- Vendor invoices; proof of delivery, installation, and payment
- New product registration and warranty documents
- Added software licenses
- Insurance renewals or coverage changes
- External correspondence
- Internal memoranda
- Current resumés of all technical and system users

The following are typical questions answered by each of these documents:

- Maintenance agreement renewals
  —What product maintenance is in effect now?
  —Is product coverage adequate?

- New-purchase related documents
  —When were new products or services purchased and who purchased them?
  —Were new purchases conditional?

- Proof of delivery or installation
  —Were new purchases received, placed into service, and paid for?

- Registration and warranty
  —Were new purchase registrations and warranty activities completed?

- Added software licenses
  —Were licenses and confirmations processed and received for all new software products?

- Insurance renewals
  —Does the current insurance coverage take into account all new purchases and returns?

- External correspondence
  —Has there been correspondence with suppliers on issues about their products after the initial purchase?
  —Are there any unresolved issues?

- Internal memoranda
  —Have internal memos or correspondence of any kind been officially exchanged regarding the system's functionality or performance?
  —Is there an electronic bulletin board or system log to which users can write or mail from their terminals?

- Users' resumés
  —What is the experience level of all technical and system users?
  —Are key support personnel backed up by "understudies?"

Conducting the Right Audit

The end result of an audit is not to get the system working or working better! The end result of an audit is the audit report.

Audit response

Your audit response must be measured by the mission you are charged with and the state you find the system in. As mentioned in chapter 1, different types of audits performed under different support conditions.

First audit.   The first audit examines a system for the first time and files a report on the starting baseline. No comparison information is provided because there was no previous baseline set to compare to. However, it is recommended that the current system be compared to the UNIX distribution only.

Routine audit.   A routine audit is a preventive measure in which a current baseline is created and compared with the previous one.

Upgrade audit.   An upgrade audit is a focused look at the current system to estimate the impact of upgrading one or more of the major software products being used. Limited baseline comparisons might be required.

Emergency audit.   An emergency audit is conducted on a system that has never been audited before and has been abandoned by key local support. It is the most difficult audit to perform.

You need to decide what approach is best for your situation. That decision depends largely on the resources available to you.

Assessing Audit Resources

After interviewing key system users and reviewing all of the pertinent documentation, assess what resources you have at your disposal and their impact on the remaining audit activities.

Prior audit history

Obviously, you'll be way out in front if you have audited this system previously or if it has been well maintained with accurate records. Remember, historical records can go a long way towards unlocking sources of help in an emergency situation where the outlook is bleak and things seem hopeless. These records can help locate key personnel in companies that are now defunct. For example, the records might contain information used to identify an individual with a unique last name who might be listed in the telephone book. That person might be able to tell you where some key employees now live or work.

Personnel

A competent system administrator who is familiar with the system and UNIX is your best asset. Another good alternative is to work with a competent UNIX system programmer.

If neither of these are available from within your organization, and you have little or no UNIX experience, you would do well to hire some temporary talent to get past the skill-level barriers you will encounter.

Status meeting

When you finish your assessment, give a more accurate and informed estimate for the remainder of your audit to the person who assigned or contracted you. Your findings to date will be appreciated and any changes in your estimate based on new information will be better received now than later.

Examination Directives

Just prior to conducting direct system examinations, be sure that the system administrator creates two full backups of the system in addition to the normal backup. Coordinate this backup with your baseline creation so that the two additional backups and the new baseline can be saved as a set.

6

Capture and Examine

Even in small UNIX installations, the number of files and directories to be examined is formidable. A knowledgeable auditor can poke around and answer a handful of specific questions. A thorough and comprehensive audit, on the other hand, requires the use of some automated procedures for the audit to be credible and timely. This book provides a set of *UNIX tools* to help you perform a comprehensive audit by recording, examining, and comparing file system information. These tools consist of programs and files that allow you to both capture and analyze information required to make informed judgments about the audited system.

This chapter describes how actual data is collected and examined for an entire UNIX file system.

The Tools

The tools consist of a number of programs and a data file that can be found in appendixes A and B of this text. You can type these scripts onto your system using the `vi` editor or you can use the card included with this text to request the programs and data file be sent to you on a high-density diskette in DOS ASCII format. It is assumed that you have a means to transfer ASCII files from a DOS diskette onto your UNIX system. All of the files contained on this diskette should be read into the `/home/baseline` directory discussed in chapter 4.

Programs

The following programs are on the diskette:

- capture
- compare
- readme.p
- di ff.p

The **capture** program collects data about all of the files and directories from the directory specified by the auditor. The **compare** program is used to compare the results of the same baseline audits captured at different times. The **readme.p** and **diff.p** programs print reports on results of the capture and compare process, respectively. All of the programs are written using the Bourne shell to ensure their compatibility with virtually all UNIX systems.

Data files are distinguished from program files by the use of capital letters. The data file included with the software is **TLIST**, which stands for "type list." The "type list" file contains ordered pairs of information used to interpret the type of file found in each directory.

capture.   The **capture** program is the audit's primary data collection tool. It is used at each audit where the current state of each UNIX directory on the system must be examined. The results of this program are stored in various data files throughout shadow directories.

The program is invoked by typing its name followed by three arguments as follows:

    capture   *directory_1 directory_2 auditname*

where

    directory_1 is the root of the directories to be examined. That is, if you wanted to audit every file in the system, you would specify directory_1 to be /. The only rule that governs this specification is that the directory must exist.

    directory_2 is the root of the baseline which is the root of the shadow directory. Rules that govern this specification are: First, the specified directory may or may not exist. Second, if the specified directory exists, the auditor will be asked if it's okay to overwrite the existing files. Based on the response to the question, the software will remove the existing specified file structure and recreate it or it will do nothing except exit **capture** and return control to the auditor at the UNIX prompt. Finally, the specified directory must not be **/home/baseline**. This directory is reserved for program and data files that are part of the audit tool set.

    auditname is the unique name assigned to the audit that you are doing.

The assumption is that multiple audits will be executed over the life of the system and that you'll want to save and be able to identify each one.

Once invoked, `capture` program performs the following functions:

- Creates a file called DIRECTORIES and places it in the baseline's root directory. This file contains a list of every subdirectory under the root directory specified for examination.

- Creates a file called README and places it in the baseline's root directory. This file contains information about the entire audit as opposed to any single directory.

- Creates a shadow directory structure and attaches it to the baseline root directory. A shadow directory will be created for every directory found in the DIRECTORIES file.

- Copies a data file called TLIST from `/home/baseline` to the baseline's root directory.

- Moves into each directory to be examined and analyzes every file it finds. The result of this intensive analysis is the creation of the README file that is placed in the examined directory's shadow directory. The README file has a fixed and variable segment. The fixed segment contains information about the directory being examined. The variable segment consists of one line of information for each file in the examined directory. The `capture` program creates one README file for every directory contained in DIRECTORIES. (The layout of the README file is included as comments in the `capture` script in appendix A.)

- Creates and maintains a LOG file that it stores in the baseline's root directory. This can be viewed or printed out using the `pr` or `lp` UNIX commands.

compare. The `compare` program is the audit's primary data comparison program. The results of this program are stored in DIFFERENCE data files throughout the shadow directories for any directory where a difference is detected. The program is invoked by typing its name followed by two arguments as follows:

`compare` *directory_1 directory_2*

where

directory_1 is the full pathname of the root of the controlling baseline directory to be examined. This is the baseline directory of the last audit.

directory_2 is the full pathname of the root of the current baseline directory just examined in this audit.

The `compare` program performs two functions:

- Compares the DIRECTORY file in each structure and writes the DIF-FERENCE file in this audit's shadow directory root directory.

- Compares the README file in each of the shadow directories. If they are equal, no action is taken. If they differ, a DIFFERENCE file is written to this audit's baseline shadow structure. The fixed segment of the README is compared and included in the DIFFERENCE file. Only files that are different, added, or deleted since the last audit are included in the variable segment of the DIFFERENCE file.

readme.p. The `readme.p` report program formats README files. It is invoked as follows:

```
readme  directory/README
```

The following is an example of the formatted output produced by this program:[*]

```
    Audit Name: FIRST      Audit Date: Mon Sep 16 15:26:11 EDT 1991
Directory Name: /etc/erm
Directory Owner: root
Directory Files: 0
  Linked Files: 0
Executable Files: 2
   Other Files: 3
Total Characters: 31561
```

```
File Details: Permissions, Owner, Group, Size, Date, Name, Chksum, Type
-rw-r- -r- -root sys 7454 4/18/90 ermes 9660 Executable
-rw-r- -r- -root sys 4507 4/18/90 ermes.c 61716 Ascii
-rw-r- -r- -root sys 8802 4/18/90 extended_ermes 14152 Executable
-rw-r- -r- -root sys 10265 4/18/90 extended_ermes.c 57937 Ascii
-rw-r- -r- -root sys 533 4/18/90 makefile 42789 Ascii
```

diff.p. The `diff.p` report program formats the DIFFERENCE file. It is invoked as follows:

```
diff.p  directory/DIFFERENCE
```

An example of the formatted output produced by this report follows:

---

[*]Because of space limitations, dates on this listing are given numerically (4/18/90) rather than spelled as they would actually appear.

```
FIRST Mon 9/16 15:26:11 EDT 1991
/etc/erm
root
0
0
2
3
31561   31571


Files That Have Changed:
-rw-r- -r- -root sys 4507 4/18/90 ermes.c 61716 Ascii
-rw-r- -r- -root sys 4517 9/11/90 ermes.c 25341 Ascii


Files That Have Been Deleted Since The Last Audit:
None


Files That Have Been Added Since The Last Audit:
None
```

Files

There are a number of data files associated with these five programming tools.

TLIST. The only data file that is used by this software is TLIST. It contains a list of ordered pairs of words:

```
executable    Executable
Terminfo      Terminfo
English            English
archive       Archive
[nt]roff      [nt]roff
ascii         Ascii
block         Block
program            Program
cannot             Cannot_Open
character     Character
commands      Commands
data               Data
directory     Directory
empty         Empty
fifo               Fifo
packed             Packed
symbolic      Link
```

The first word of each pair is unique text found in the output of the UNIX **file** command. The second word of each pair is the single descriptive word used by the **capture** program to describe the type of file analyzed.

The programs described in this section create data files in the baseline root directory in addition to README and DIFFERENCE files they create throughout the shadow directories. The **capture** program creates README, DIRECTORIES, and LOG.

README. The README file in the baseline's root is different than the README files written throughout the shadow directories in that it describes information that is common to the entire audit and the entire system. The following gives an example of the contents of this file:

```
Audit Name: FIRST  Time: Tue Sep 17 13:26:27 EDT 1991
Root Directory Examined: /
Root Directory of Baseline: /usr/audits/1991
Count of Directories in Baseline: 329 /usr/audits/1991 /DIRECTORIES
UNIX Kernel File Name: dgux
UNIX Version: Pass Y (starter)
UNIX Release Number: 4.31.
System Node Name: no_node
UNIX Machine Name: Aviion
System Free Space by File System
logical: / Physical: (/dev/dsk/root 26610 blocks 5272 files
logical: /usr Physical: (/dev/dsk/usr 569 blocks 206 files
Total Blocks Used by All File Systems: 775
```

This file answers big picture questions about the audit like these:

- What was the name assigned to this audit and when was the audit done?
- What directories were examined and where was the shadow stored?
- How many directories were analyzed and what were their names?
- What was the UNIX version number and on what machine was the audit performed?
- How much free space was there at the time of the audit?
- How many blocks were in use at the time of the audit?

DIRECTORIES. The DIRECTORIES file is created at the very beginning of the capture process. It is a list of all of the directories in the system you are auditing that are found below the root directory you specify for examination. An example of the contents of this file is as follows:

```
/admin
/dev
/dev/dsk
```

```
/dev/pdsk
/dev/rdsk
/dev/rmt
/dev/rpdsk
/etc
/etc/domain
/etc/erm
/etc/init.d
/etc/log
/etc/rc0.d
/etc/rc1.d
/etc/rc2.d
/etc/rc3.d
/etc/rc4.d
/etc/rc5.d
/etc/rc6.d
/etc/rcS.d
/etc/sm
/etc/sm.bak
/etc/sysadm
/etc/uucp
/etc/yp
/etc/yp/binding
...etc
```

LOG.   The LOG file gets created and appended to on a regular basis during the time **capture** is being executed. A partial sample of the contents of the LOG file is shown here:

```
Tue Sep 17 13:26:28 EDT 1991 Begin Listing Dirs to be examined.
Tue Sep 17 13:26:46 EDT 1991 End Listing Dirs to be examined.
Tue Sep 17 13:26:46 EDT 1991 Begin Count of Dirs in Base Line:
Tue Sep 17 13:26:46 EDT 1991 End Count of Dirs in Base Line:
Tue Sep 17 13:27:03 EDT 1991 Creating Shadow Directories:
Tue Sep 17 13:27:55 EDT 1991 End of Shadow Directory Creation:
Tue Sep 17 13:27:56 EDT 1991 Begin Directory Examinations
Tue Sep 17 13:27:56 EDT 1991 Directory Name: /admin
Tue Sep 17 13:29:23 EDT 1991 Directory Name: /dev
Tue Sep 17 13:51:24 EDT 1991 Directory Name: /dev/dsk
Tue Sep 17 13:51:41 EDT 1991 Directory Name: /dev/pdsk
Tue Sep 17 13:52:03 EDT 1991 Directory Name: /dev/rdsk
Tue Sep 17 13:52:17 EDT 1991 Directory Name: /dev/rmt
Tue Sep 17 13:52:35 EDT 1991 Directory Name: /dev/rpdsk
Tue Sep 17 13:52:53 EDT 1991 Directory Name: /etc
Tue Sep 17 13:59:16 EDT 1991 Directory Name: /etc/domain
Tue Sep 17 13:59:17 EDT 1991 Directory Name: /etc/erm
Tue Sep 17 13:59:53 EDT 1991 Directory Name: /etc/init.d
```

```
Tue Sep 17 13:59:54 EDT 1991 Directory Name: /etc/log
Tue Sep 17 14:00:17 EDT 1991 Directory Name: /etc/rc0.d
Tue Sep 17 14:00:34 EDT 1991 Directory Name: /etc/rc1.d
Tue Sep 17 14:00:51 EDT 1991 Directory Name: /etc/rc2.d
Tue Sep 17 14:01:08 EDT 1991 Directory Name: /etc/rc3.d
Tue Sep 17 14:01:26 EDT 1991 Directory Name: /etc/rc4.d
Tue Sep 17 14:01:44 EDT 1991 Directory Name: /etc/rc5.d
Tue Sep 17 14:02:02 EDT 1991 Directory Name: /etc/rc6.d
Tue Sep 17 14:02:20 EDT 1991 Directory Name: /etc/rcs.d
Tue Sep 17 14:02:37 EDT 1991 Directory Name: /etc/sm
Tue Sep 17 14:02:38 EDT 1991 Directory Name: /etc/sm.bak
Tue Sep 17 14:02:39 EDT 1991 Directory Name: /etc/sysadm
Tue Sep 17 14:04:16 EDT 1991 Directory Name: /etc/uucp
Tue Sep 17 14:06:46 EDT 1991 Directory Name: /etc/yp
Tue Sep 17 14:06:47 EDT 1991 Directory Name: /etc/yp/binding
...etc
Total Directories Processed: 328   Total Files Processed: 5286
```

Procedures

The typical procedure for using this software would be to use an existing directory structure that is dedicated to the audit function. In this way, you can load in the last or even the entire set of baseline shadows for all previous audits if broader comparisons are useful. For example, consider the directory structure shown in Figure 6.1. In this example, previous audits used the year as the name of the baseline's root directory. Continuing this convention makes a lot of sense.

You will need between one-half and two megabytes of disk memory to store the output generated by capture, depending on the logical size of your file systems. Once the baseline directory for this audit is chosen, the entire system should be analyzed using the capture program as follows:

```
capture / /usr/audits/1992 ANNUAL92 > ERRORLOG 2>&1
```

This program will run for hours depending on the size of the system you are auditing and the speed of the processor(s). For that reason, it is a good idea to run the job in the background, or if you are initiating the process remotely, to use the "no hangup" (nohup) feature. In all cases it would be a good idea to redirect "standard output" and any error messages into a temporary file (*ERRORLOG*) in case the program does not run to completion as expected. The following is an example of the same command using nohup:

```
nohup capture / /usr/audits/1992 ANNUAL92 > ERRORLOG 2>&1
```

In each case, the ampersand (&) causes the job to run in the background. Standard output messages and error messages that would normally have

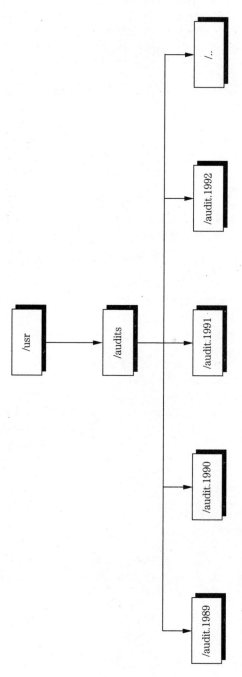

Figure 6.1 Comparing annual audits.

come to your terminal are redirected to the ERRORLOG file and can be printed out after the program finishes.

If you want to monitor the progress of **capture** you can invoke it and **tee** the output so progress messages come to your screen and get recorded in a file you choose. For example, consider the following:

```
capture / /usr/audits/1992 ANNUAL92 2> ERRORLOG | tee MYLOG
```

In this example the ampersand is not used because the program will be sending a stream of output to your terminal on a regular basis.

The capture process is slow, but it is methodical and comprehensive. Run the process at night, if possible, and pick up the results in the morning. The baseline by itself is not very useful other than as a catalog of all the directories in the system. The primary use of the baseline is as the benchmark comparison with previous or future baseline data sets.

If you are doing the very first audit on a system using the **capture** program, be sure that you follow the steps outlined in chapter 4. That is, go through the process of doing a full UNIX restore using the current UNIX distribution directly from the original media. Run **capture** on the newly restored distribution only, in order to distinguish the initial system from the current system. This is an essential step if your conclusions about the integrity of the current system are to have a strong foundation. Save this initial baseline to removable media and restore the production system. Then run **capture** on the restored system and save the results in a different baseline directory.

If you are conducting a full file system audit, you should copy some sensitive files from the **/etc** directory to its shadow directory after the capture process. These are the files in **/etc** to copy:

```
fstab
group
gettydefs
inittab
passwd
profile
```

At this point the structure of your system should look something like Figure 6.2. You are now ready to compare the last baseline with the current baseline.

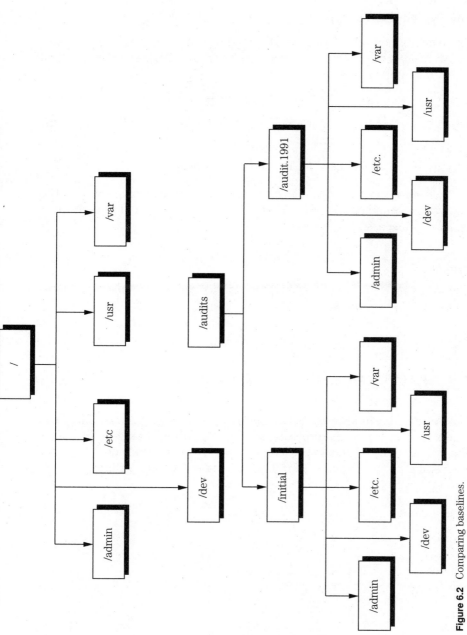

Figure 6.2 Comparing baselines.

File System Examination

The examination of a UNIX file system should answer basic questions as well as pose questions to be answered. Simply stated, the examination tries to determine the following:

- Is the system secure?
- Can changes in the system since the last audit be reasonably explained?
- Are the system's resources adequate?
- Is the system being used for its intended purpose?

Furthermore, the objective measurements and comparisons made on the file system should corroborate information provided to you during the user interviews discussed in chapter 5.

Security

The following aspects of UNIX system security can be examined by a careful look at the file system:

- Passwords
- File and directory permissions
- Unexplained command file changes

Passwords. Basic security is controlled by the /etc/passwd file. Let's take a look at it and its directory. A copy of the file should be in /etc's shadow directory. The following commands change to the shadow directory and send a copy of the passwd file to the system's default printer:

```
cd /usr/audits/1991/etc
lp passwd

root::0:1:  Special Admin login:/:/sbin/sh
sysadm::0:0: Regular Admin login:/admin:/sbin/sh
daemon:*:1:1: Daemon Login for daemons needing
permissions:/:/sbin/sh
bin:*:2:2:  Admin :/bin:
sys:*:3:3:  Admin :/usr/src:
adm:*:4:4:  Admin :/usr/adm:/sbin/sh
uucp:*:5:5:  UUCP Login:/usr/spool/uucp:/usr/lib/uucp /uucico
nuucp:*:5:1: UUCP Admin Login :/usr/lib/uucp:/sbin/sh
lp:*:6:2:   Printer:/usr/lib:/sbin/sh
mail:*:8:1:  Sendmail Login for mail
```

```
delivery:/usr/mail:/usr/bin/mail
sync::19:1:   Disk Update Login without password:/:/bin/sync
yp:*:37:37:   YP Admin :/usr/etc/yp:/sbin/sh
nfs:*:38:38: NFS Admin :/:/sbin/sh
ftp:*:39:39: FTP guest Login:/var/ftp:/sbin/sh
nobody:*:65534:65534::/:
+:
```

The password file contains a separate record for each user permitted to log in. Each record is contained on a separate line, and each field in the record is separated by a colon. The second field on each line should contain an encrypted password value, and should never be empty. Analysis of this file indicates that there is no password protection for two account logins: *root* and *sysadm*.

Other fields of interest in this directory are fields 5 and 6. Field 5 designates the account's home directory. Field 6 designates an account's optional startup software.

Printing out a copy of the README file in the /etc shadow directory yields the following:

```
readme.p | lp
```

```
Audit Name: AUDIT_01       Audit Date: Mon Sep 23 08:18:01 EDT 1991
      Directory Name: /etc
      Directory Owner: root
      Directory Files: 17
         Linked Files: 59
Executable Files: 0
         Other Files: 51
Total Characters: 3588200
```

```
File Details: Permissions, Owner, Group, Size, Date, Name, Chksum, Type
-rw-r- -r- -root sys 276 Aug 19 14:57 TIMEZONE 23548 English
-rw-r- -r- -root sys 273 Aug 19 14:57 TIMEZONE.csh 23322 English
-rw-r- -r- -root sys 273 Apr 18 1990 TIMEZONE.csh.proto 23322 English
-rw-r- -r- -root sys 276 Apr 18 1990 TIMEZONE.proto 23548 English
-r- -r- -r- -bin 2114 Apr 18 1990 ascii 64151 Ascii
lrwxrwxrwx root other 19 Aug 19 14:35 bcs_cat 60721 Link
lrwxrwxrwx root other 21 Aug 19 14:35 bcs_match 20046 Link
lrwxrwxrwx root other 16 Aug 19 13:23 berk_dump 45800 Link
lrwxrwxrwx root other 18 Aug 19 13:23 chroot 873 Link
lrwxrwxrwx root other 20 Aug 19 13:23 ckbupscd 38326 Link
lrwxrwxrwx root other 16 Aug 19 13:23 clri 7840 Link
lrwxrwxrwx root other 18 Aug 19 13:23 config 58576 Link
lrwxrwxrwx root other 16 Aug 19 13:23 cron 2037 Link
lrwxrwxrwx root other 19 Aug 19 13:23 deblock 43667 Link
```

```
-rw-r- -r- -root 1790 Aug 19 15:00 devlinktab 65125 English
lrwxrwxrwx root other 17 Aug 19 13:23 devnm 15250 Link
lrwxrwxrwx root other 13 Aug 19 13:23 df 56123 Link
lrwxrwxrwx root other 19 Aug 19 13:23 dg_fsdb 3621 Link
-rw-r- -r- -root sys 7159 Sep 7 18:12 dgux.params 31628 Ascii
-rw-r- -r- -root sys 7161 Apr 18 1990 dgux.params.proto 31778 Ascii
-rw-r- -r- -root sys 220 Apr 18 1990 dgux.prototab 20479 Ascii
-rw-r- -r- -root sys 3445 Aug 19 14:56 dgux.rclktab 20779 Ascii
-rw-r- -r- -root sys 3445 Apr 18 1990 dgux.rclktab.proto 20779 Ascii
lrwxrwxrwx root other 16 Aug 19 13:23 dump 45800 Link
lrwxrwxrwx root other 17 Aug 19 13:23 dump2 50971 Link
-rw-r- -r- -root sys 0 Aug 19 14:56 dumpdates 0 Empty
-rw-r- -r- -root sys 0 Apr 18 1990 dumpdates.proto 0 Empty
lrwxrwxrwx root other 18 Aug 19 13:23 dumpfs 43609 Link
-rw-r- -r- -root sys 736 Aug 19 14:56 dumptab 50579 Ascii
-rw-r- -r- -bin 736 Aug 28 1990 dumptab.proto 50579 Ascii
lrwxrwxrwx root other 20 Aug 19 13:23 filesave 24199 Link
lrwxrwxrwx root other 12 Aug 19 14:35 fsck 39251 Link
lrwxrwxrwx root other 16 Aug 19 13:23 fsdb 59530 Link
-rw-rw-rw- root 568 Aug 19 14:55 fstab 48512 English
-rw-r- -r- -root sys 568 Apr 18 1990 fstab.proto 48512 English
lrwxrwxrwx root other 17 Aug 19 13:23 fuser 21095 Link
lrwxrwxrwx root other 17 Aug 19 13:23 getty 23491 Link
-rw-r- -r- -root sys 2435 Aug 19 14:56 gettydefs 29419 English
-rw-r- -r- -root sys 2435 Apr 18 1990 gettydefs.proto 29419 English
-rw-r- -r- -root sys 213 Aug 19 14:56 group 17890 Ascii
-rw-r- -r- -root sys 213 Apr 18 1990 group.proto 17890 Ascii
lrwxrwxrwx root other 17 Aug 19 13:23 grpck 64221 Link
lrwxrwxrwx root other 12 Aug 19 13:23 halt 3454 Link
lrwxrwxrwx root other 16 Aug 19 13:23 helpadm Link
-rw-r- -r- -root bin 0 Aug 24 16:49 hosts 0 Empty
lrwxrwxrwx root other 12 Aug 19 13:23 init 52580 Link
-rw-r- -r- -root 914 Sep 13 10:36 inittab 8901 Ascii
-rw-r- -r- -root sys 857 Apr 18 1990 inittab.proto 4427 Ascii
lrwxrwxrwx root other 19 Aug 19 13:23 install 9099 Link
-rw-r- -r- -root 54 Sep 23 08:06 ioctl.syscon 3394 Ascii
-rw-r- -r- -root sys 37 Aug 19 14:56 issue 2995 Ascii
lrwxrwxrwx root other 19 Aug 19 13:23 killall 44349 Link
lrwxrwxrwx root other 19 Aug 19 13:23 labelit 9769 Link
lrwxrwxrwx root other 16 Aug 19 13:23 link 10099 Link
-rw-r- -r- -root sys 637 Aug 19 14:56 login.csh 51828 Ascii
-rw-r- -r- -root sys 637 Apr 18 1990 login.csh.proto 51828 Ascii
lrwxrwxrwx root other 16 Aug 19 13:23 magic 27190 Link
lrwxrwxrwx root other 17 Aug 19 13:23 mknod 21711 Link
-rw-r- -r- -root 60 Sep 23 08:06 mnttab 4774 Ascii
-rw-r- -r- -root sys 0 Apr 18 1990 mnttab.proto 0 Empty
-rw-r- -r- -root sys 626 Aug 19 14:56 motd 28941 Ascii
-rw-r- -r- -root sys 626 Apr 18 1990 motd.proto 28941 Ascii
```

```
lrwxrwxrwx root other 13 Aug 19 13:23 mount 27556 Link
lrwxrwxrwx root other 17 Aug 19 13:23 mvdir 40417 Link
lrwxrwxrwx root other 18 Aug 19 13:23 ncheck 3559 Link
-rw-r- -r- -root bin 0 Aug 24 16:49 networks 0 Empty
-r- -r- -r- -root sys 708 Aug 19 14:56 passwd 57159 Ascii
-rw-r- -r- -root sys 708 Aug 28 1990 passwd.proto 57159 Ascii
lrwxrwxrwx root other 17 Aug 19 13:23 prfdc 64153 Link
lrwxrwxrwx root other 17 Aug 19 13:23 prfld 27345 Link
lrwxrwxrwx root other 17 Aug 19 13:23 prfpr 1357 Link
lrwxrwxrwx root other 19 Aug 19 13:23 prfsnap 45894 Link
lrwxrwxrwx root other 19 Aug 19 13:23 prfstat 5607 Link
-rw-r- -r- -root sys 886 Aug 19 14:56 printcap 10583 Ascii
-rw-r- -r- -root bin 886 Apr 18 1990 printcap.proto 10583 Ascii
-rw-r- -r- -root sys 1158 Aug 19 14:56 profile 24383 Ascii
-rw-r- -r- -root sys 1158 May 15 1990 profile.proto 24383 Ascii
-rw-rw-r- -root sys 7939 Sep 23 08:07 ps_data 825 Data
lrwxrwxrwx root other 16 Aug 19 13:23 pwck 19808 Link
lrwxrwxrwx root other 18 Aug 19 13:23 rename 2468 Link
lrwxrwxrwx root other 18 Aug 19 13:23 renice 62991 Link
lrwxrwxrwx root other 19 Aug 19 13:23 restore 42917 Link
lrwxrwxrwx root other 18 Aug 19 13:23 setmnt 49202 Link
lrwxrwxrwx root other 16 Aug 19 13:23 shutdown 25018 Link
-rw-r- -r- -root sys 437 Aug 19 14:57 stdlogin 36904 Ascii
-rw-r- -r- -root sys 437 Apr 18 1990 stdlogin.proto 36904 Ascii
-rw-r- -r- -root sys 507 Aug 19 14:57 stdprofile 41707 Ascii
-rw-r- -r- -root sys 507 Apr 18 1990 stdprofile.proto 41707 Ascii
lrwxrwxrwx root other 18 Aug 19 13:23 swapon 57351 Link
lrwxrwxrwx root other 18 Aug 19 13:23 sysdef 51377 Link
-rw-r- -r- -root sys 448 Aug 19 14:57 syslog.conf 37014 Ascii
-rw-r- -r- -root sys 448 Apr 18 1990 syslog.conf.proto 37014 Ascii
-rw-rw-rw- root 4 Sep 23 08:07 syslog.pid 165 Ascii
lrwxrwxrwx root other 19 Aug 19 13:23 syslogd 19780 Link
lrwxrwxrwx root other 20 Aug 19 13:23 systemid 3361 Link
lrwxrwxrwx root other 20 Aug 19 13:23 tapesave 25197 Link
lrwxrwxrwx root other 12 Aug 19 13:23 telinit 52580 Link
lrwxrwxrwx root other 18 Aug 19 13:23 termcap 196 Link
lrwxrwxrwx root other 18 Aug 19 13:23 tunefs 52869 Link
lrwxrwxrwx root other 14 Aug 19 13:23 umount 15882 Link
lrwxrwxrwx root other 18 Aug 19 13:23 unlink 11255 Link
lrwxrwxrwx root other 18 Aug 19 13:23 update 30552 Link
-rw-r- -r- -root sys 576 Sep 23 08:28 utmp 16903 Data
-rw-rw- -r- -root sys 0 Apr 18 1990 utmp.proto 0 Empty
lrwxrwxrwx root other 16 Aug 19 13:23 vipw 41953 Link
lrwxrwxrwx root other 19 Aug 19 13:23 volcopy 53243 Link
lrwxrwxrwx root other 16 Aug 19 13:23 wall 13578 Link
lrwxrwxrwx root other 17 Aug 19 13:23 whodo 38698 Link
-rw-rw-r- -adm 24320 Sep 23 08:28 wtmp 63534 Data
-rw-r- -r- -adm 0 Apr 18 1990 wtmp.proto 0 Empty
```

One of the directory entries in this file merits particular attention:

```
-r- -r- -r- -root sys 708 Aug 19 14:56 passwd 57159 Ascii
```

This entry indicates that ownership (`root`) and permissions (`-r–r–r–`) are correct and when the last change to the password file was made. A typical audit conclusion would be as follows:

1. This UNIX system is totally vulnerable because the most important users have no passwords.
2. The permissions are correct, preventing anyone other than `root` from directly modifying the password file.
3. The last time someone changed a password entry in this file was on 8ust 19 at 14:56 of the current year.
4. You can't know if the two entries without passwords were ever entered or removed.

Of course you'd recommend that passwords be assigned immediately. Also, if 8ust was more than a few months ago, you would recommend that all passwords be changed.

Permissions. Files and directories are assigned permissions directly using the `chmod` command, or indirectly by a user's `umask` whenever that user creates a new file. You'll want to inspect the system to judge if there is a balanced approach to permission restrictions. If permissions are too restrictive more people are likely to need or want access to the root password. If permissions are too liberal, system files are vulnerable to undesirable or malicious changes. Eric Foxley's discussion on this topic are notable (from *UNIX for Super Users* published by Addison-Wesley, pages 133 and 134):

Command Permissions

With a few exceptions listed below and elsewhere, all system commands (all files in directories `/usr` and `/usr/bin`) should have an access mode such as 771 (for binary programs) or 775 (for shell scripts), to ensure no public write permission, and no public read permission except where necessary (for shell scripts). The group permissions should be set so that the users with permissions to change to the system administration group can perform system changes without need for the "super-user" status; if this arrangement is not used, the modes should be set to 711 and 755 respectively. If the execution of shell scripts does not require read permission, then they should be with mode 771; read permission should in general be avoided, to prevent people from taking copies of programs or shell scripts to, for example, a floppy disk attached to a terminal....

Root-owned Writeable Files

There should be no root-owned public-writeable files.

Directory Permissions

Directories such as /bin should not have public write permission. It is surprising how many managers carefully check the access permissions on the files in their main directories, but do not check the directories themselves. If there exists public write permission on the directory, users can then save a copy of a command in their own directory, delete the original, and insert a replacement of the same name. The command to check the permission on a directory is for example:

```
ls -ld /bin/usr/bin
```

A suitable mode would be 775, to allow them to be searchable and readable by the public.

In general each user's home directory, .profile and .login files should be owned by that user, and should have write permission only to that user, for similar reasons to those above.

Command file contents. An important part of the security examination is to determine if a UNIX program has been changed in an unauthorized manner. One of the reasons for recording detail aspects of each file is to determine if there are any changes in files that should never or rarely change. To this end, the 16-bit checksum is recorded for each file in order to detect subtle changes in file content. While this check is not foolproof, it relies on the general principle that an overt replacement of a UNIX command with an illicit program with the same name is not likely to have the same

- Distribution date
- Number of characters
- Checksum of file contents

Auditing a system consistently from the original distribution requires the examination of all changes. This examination makes sense, and for the most part, once the changes that occur from an older baseline to the current one can be explained, the current baseline is accepted as the new standard and it is stored away to be used as the reference for the next audit. If the changes can't be explained, they are evidence of a problem that needs attention. After the problems are resolved another baseline should be captured that will be used as the standard for the next audit.

The `compare` program is used to define any changes between the last baseline and the current one. The following is a typical invocation of `compare`:

```
compare /usr/audits/1990 /usr/audits/1991
```

The `compare` program would compare each of the audits and report any differences by reading the README files in each of the audit's shadow directories and writing the differences into DIFFERENCE files in the current audit's shadow directory. The following is an example of a DIFFERENCE file:

```
FIRST Mon Sep 16 15:26:11 EDT 1991 ; Name of this Audit
/etc/erm    ; Directory That Changed
root                 ; Directory Owners Compared
0            ; Directory Files Compared
0   0        ; Linked Files Compared
2   2        ; Executable Files Compared
3   3        ; Other Files Compared
31561   31571       ; Tot. Characters Compared


Files That Have Changed: _____
-rw-r- -r- -root sys 4507 Apr 18 1990 ermes.c 61716 Ascii ;Old
-rw-r- -r- -root sys 4517 Sep 11 1990 ermes.c 25341 Ascii ; New
Files That Have Been Deleted Since The Last Audit:_____
None


Files That Have Been Added Since The Last Audit: _____
None
```

Resources

The examination of resources primarily deals with space allocation in file systems. While it is simple enough to check free space with the **df** command or current file usage with **du**, the auditor must determine if the space used or not used is reasonable based on the intended use of the system. Space is consumed by data storage on systems in two main ways:

- Through natural growth of legitimate information that must be retained online for rapid access
- Through the proliferation of copies of data files or outdated application system images that should really be stored offline if at all

Legitimate data growth should be estimated. In most databases there is a relationship between measurable external events and measurable data growth. These relationships are generally expressed in record relationships.

From the current size of the records, you can make a gross projection of size. Appendix D gives an example of relationship definitions and sizing. In that example, the external relationships are described by the business owners. These are shown on the first page under "Data Entity Assump-tions." That information is then used to drive the number of records in each database table, and in turn to produce a sizing estimate that is fairly accurate.

Proliferation of unnecessary copies of data is common on systems where technicians still play an active role or where the systems administrator is not well-trained. Copies of old versions of software and/or data used to demonstrate or troubleshoot applications is fairly common. Examining volume by user account generally reveals these types of abuses.

To find out the total number of characters used by each user account in the system you can issue the following command line:

```
find / -user accountname -print | wc
```

This command locates the full pathname of every file in the system owned by the specified *accountname* and counts the characters in each. The wc provides a total of all characters after the last file's count has been displayed.

Usage

Printing a copy of the /etc/group file gives some indication of group access, as shown:

```
lp /usr/audits/1991/etc/group

root::0:root
other::1:
bin::2:root,bin,daemon
sys::3:root,bin,sys,adm
adm::4:root,adm,daemon
mail::5:mail,bin
lp::6:lp
uucp::8:uucp
daemon::12:root,daemon
operator::18:adm
nfs::38:nfs
ftp::39:ftp
general::100:
+
```

This file together with the passwd file will give you a good idea of who has access to what. There are three telltale signs of users using the system outside the bounds intended for them:

1. Account names appear as members of groups to which they shouldn't belong.

2. There is mixed user file ownership in the same directory.

3. Permissions of normally restricted UNIX commands differ from the distribution.

If the system activity reporting process is active, usage can be very accurately determined down to which user used which commands on any given day. The following chapter discusses system activity reporting in greater detail.

7

System Response

Chapters 5 and 6 focus the audit on the "static" aspects of your system. This chapter focuses attention on the dynamic aspects of interactive system response. Years ago, IBM published a research article that correlated response time delays to interruption and distraction, especially for "knowledge" workers. There is no doubt that an interactive system that hesitates to interact requires an undue amount of attention to deal with the problem of when to "go to the next step." As this hesitation gets worse, workers start to find ways around the system so they can get their work done in a timely way.

The audit should review and address response time issues. It should identify problems and probe likely causes for further investigation.

Signs

Response time specifications are often an essential part of contract performance when purchasing a system from a computer manufacturer or value-added reseller. RFPs often contain system performance requirements like the following:

> *The system must take no longer than one second to respond to an interactive request to fetch and display information based on keyed (indexed) data 95 percent of the time.*

Today's technology makes this requirement realistic. In the simple case where a company is using a computer for telemarketing or sales order entry of any kind, the last thing anyone wants is to tell anxious buyers that they must wait for computer response. Furthermore, calling habits of telephone-based consumers predict that they will call in fairly narrow windows. Business consumers are likely to call around 10 A.M. and 2 P.M. Retail consumers are likely to call around 8 A.M., noon, or 7 P.M. For commercial applications, morning groupings will tend to be earlier after weekends and holidays or at the beginning and end of natural product sales cycles. Concurrent demands such as these create peak load conditions.

How will you know if response times are meeting user expectations heavy system loading? The most obvious way to detect a response problem is to ask system users. Don't be content with what you are told by system administrators or user department supervisors. Ask or observe line workers directly. Ask the same questions about different times of the day, week, or month.

Another sign of poor response time might be a pending upgrade request. This is often the first and only response to poor performance.

Multiple logins are usually sure signs of response-time problem workarounds. Users who log in to more than one terminal at one time are generally trying to increase their work throughput.

Causes and Remedies

Determining the likely causes and probable remedies for poor system response time requires measurement and experience. On a multi-user system where many different kinds of activities are going on at once, determining the exact cause of slow response for one or more types of users can be tricky. Furthermore, there are no "sure fire" remedies like using a faster computer or adding more memory or disk resource for some response-time problems. Your goal should be to determine the extent of the response problem and research the probable cause and remedy. You do not need to be a system performance "expert" or technician. Your objective, as always, is to *uncover, report, and recommend.*

UNIX itself has accounting programs that monitor system usage and performance. These should be used in addition to more subjective reports (from interviews) to establish or corroborate likely causes or remedies for poor system performance.

UNIX Accounting

The accounting software that comes with UNIX systems needs to be explicitly turned on. This software is not an inherent part of the UNIX operating system; it is optional. Ideally the site administrator has been using the accounting software and printing out its regular hardcopy reports for some time prior to the audit. If this is not the case or the accounting software is not turned on, get the system administrator to activate it. On recent systems there is a menu option associated with the systems administration shell software. Otherwise you can turn on system accounting by placing an appropriate entry in an `rc` file and `cron` table.

In general, UNIX accounting software does the following things:

- Collects and saves information about user connect times and system usage (commands used)
- Collects and saves information about system events (date changes, shutdowns and reboots)
- Responds to report requests about information it has collected
- Summarizes daily information into monthly reports, which it makes available upon requests
- Automatically clears out daily information after it creates monthly summaries

The following directories are used by the accounting software to save and process collected information:

`/var/adm/acct/nite` Contains files used for daily processing. (For older systems, replace `/var` with `/usr`.)

`/var/adm/acct/sum` Contains summary files.

`/var/adm/acct/fiscal` Contains related resource charge-back details if that option is used.

UNIX accounting reports

The best way to gauge the usefulness of UNIX accounting software is to understand the three reports that are made available by this software:

- Daily line usage report
- Daily usage by login name
- Daily and monthly command totals

Daily line usage report. The following information is available from this report:

- *Reporting interval.* The "from" and "to" dates included in this report.
- *System events.* The number of shutdowns, reboots, and recoveries during the reporting interval.
- *System duration.* The total number of minutes in the reporting interval.
  This information is followed by a table showing the following information for each line or port on the system:

—*Line*. Identifies the port being reported on (tty or console).

—*Minutes*. The total minutes connected during the reporting interval.

—*Percent*. The percentage of lines connected for use during the total reporting interval.

—# *Sess*. The number of times a port was accessed for connection.

—# *On*. The number of times a port was used to log a user into the system.

—# *Off*. The number of times a user logged off plus any interrupts on this line.

Some of the questions answered by this report are as follows:

1. Which users avail themselves of system resources the most? Obviously, you can't use the system if you're not logged in. However, simply being logged in does not ensure that a user is actually doing anything.

2. Do users leave their terminals open and accessible for others to use? If a user logs in once and logs off once and uses 400 minutes of connect time each day, it's a good bet that he or she leaves the terminal unattended.

3. Is a line chattering? Faulty software matching (between data bits, stop bits, and parity settings) on serial lines or faulty cables or multiplexers can cause false system interrupts which can have a noticeable and severe impact on system performance.

Daily usage by login name. The accounting system summarizes information on each 24-hour basis according to parameters established by the system administrator. The "daily usage by login name" report contains information about these daily summaries. The following information is available from this report:

- *Date and time*. The end time of the 24-hour reporting period included in this report.

- *UID*. A unique number assigned by the system administrator to anyone having rights to log in to the system.

- *Login name*. The login account name.

- *CPU minutes*. CPU time used by this login name during the reporting period. Two columns are dedicated to this information: prime time and non-prime time minutes. Prime time and non-prime time are established by the system's administrator.

- *Kcore-mins*. Total memory in kilobytes used per minute. This measurement, like the last, is also reported on for prime time and non-prime time minutes.

- *Connect minutes*. How long this login was logged onto the system, again in prime time and non-prime time minutes.

- *Disk blocks.* The total amount of temporary disk space used by this user during the reporting interval.

- *# of processes.* The number of processes invoked by the user for all log-in sessions in the reporting interval.

- *# of sessions.* The number of times the user logged into the system during the reporting interval.

- *# of disk samples.* The number of times the disk accounting was run to obtain the average number of disk blocks.

- *Fee.* The total charges to the user for this reporting interval.

This report provides any given day's activities at the user level. Use it when users have complaints about a specific date that they can identify. Questions answered by this report include the following:

1. How balanced is the usage of system resources between prime and non-prime time?
2. Which user consumed the most resources: CPU, memory, and disk?

Daily and monthly command totals. Daily and monthly command summaries use the same format. Daily reports print information about the date requested. Monthly reports print information from the last date the monthly accounting software was run until the time of the report request (the activity to date). The following information is available from this report:

- *Command name.* The name of the command. All shell programs are reported under their respective shell invocations (`sh, csh, ksh`).

- *Numbers commands.* The number of times a command was invoked.

- *Total Kcore-mins.* The total kilobytes of memory used by a process per minute during its execution.

- *Total CPU minutes.* The total processing time for all executions of this command during the reporting period.

- *Total real minutes.* The total real-time minutes (clock time) this process has run.

- *Mean size Kcore-mins.* The total Kcore-mins divided by the total CPU minutes.

- *Hog factor.* A ratio of system availability to system usage; that is, the total available CPU time that the process used.

- *Chars transferred.* The number of characters handled by *read* and *write* system calls.

- *Blocks read.* The total physical block read and writes that a process performed.

Questions answered by this report include the following:

1. What commands are being executed most by this system?
2. What are the effects of each command on the system?

System activity reports (SAR)

System activity reports or *SARs* are a finer set of measurement reports available on System V UNIX systems. If the system administrator runs these reports regularly, he or she is likely to know of performance degradation before users realize it and start to complain.

These reports allow you to focus on specific aspects of hardware usage with much greater precision than system accounting reports. SAR reporting is discussed in detail, along with plenty of examples and detailed explanations, in *System Performance Tuning* by Mike Loukides (published by O'Reilly and Associates).

Of the 20 or so available SAR reports, the following are the most useful in helping to detect possible causes of unacceptable system response:

```
sar -A  Reports all activity data
sar -b  Reports buffer cache usage and hit rate
sar -u  Reports CPU utilization
sar -w  Reports swapping and paging activity
```

Inadequate Hardware Resources

If the computer's equipment resources are not adequate, sluggish performance is always the result. It can be hard to determine, though, whether the hardware resources are adequate and sluggishness is due to some other reason. When inspecting a system, follow the leads of known external usage. For example, a system that is used for intensive calculations or graphic imaging is more likely to be short on CPU or memory than a relational database system. Or suppose a system must respond to different classes of usage: interactive, batch, and real time. In this example, interactive response could easily be overwhelmed by one or a combination of simultaneous batch or real time processing.

The main factors associated with a computer's strength are as follows:

- CPU capability and clock speed
- Amount of cache and main RAM
- Number, speed, and efficiency of attached disks and controllers
- Bandwidth of inter-device data buses
- Intelligence and buffer capacities of terminal line controllers

Compromising Software

Regardless of the speed and efficiency of the computer equipment in use, a system can have miserable response time due to bad software utilization. For example, a database application that is poorly suited to how the data is accessed might force frequent retrievals based on sequential searches instead of indexed ones. Or a system with many users might be sharing an application where the code needs to be interpreted each time it is used, or in which the authors of the software have made little or no use of shared text segments and other semaphore-related efficiencies.

A multi-tasking environment often gives rise to products that preempt resources needed by other concurrent products. For these reasons, your first response to poor performance should not be to upgrade your hardware—it might not help.

If the operating system software is not the latest revision from the computer manufacturer, try to get your hands on the release note features of each version between what you are running and the latest. Release notes might indicate that either corrections or enhancements have been made since the outdated UNIX version and some more recent version.

Hidden Interrupts

Sometimes, strange things occur that cause a system to lose processing power for no apparent reason. A bad communication device or cable can cause rapid port interrupts, causing the system to respond as if logins were being attempted. This is as close as a commercial UNIX system comes to processing real time events, to which most UNIX systems are not well-suited.

Poor Resource Planning

There are two issues to consider when managing existing resources on a UNIX system: the logical assignment of physical resources and how the operating system is tuned for any specific application.

When it comes to assigning physical resources, a commonsense approach to what is kept memory-resident and how information is balanced or stripped across available disks can have a dramatic impact on how well or poorly a system responds. Another resource assignment issue is the size of directories and the number of paths that must be searched in order to find requested software. As a general rule, there should be no more than 50 files in any directory that is searched for an executable file. Furthermore, the most frequently used executable files should be placed at the beginning of the directory in which they exist. Similarly, the most frequently searched directory should be placed at the beginning of the user's path.

The mapping of a logical disk block to more than one physical disk block is a feature available on most UNIX systems for the past few years. This feature allows a system administrator to trade off disk space to gain speed. That is, whenever a block is read, the operating system can have access to one, two, four, eight, or 16 blocks (with 512 characters per block). Depending on how the system is used, one of these choices will be an optimal compromise between speed and wasting unused disk space. If the factor is too large, considerable disk space can be wasted.

On the tuning side, issues like specifying too few buffers for too many users can bring a system to its knees, regardless of how much physical memory is available.

Physical assignment and tuning must be addressed before considering any kind of system upgrade. In fact, even if you're certain that a hardware upgrade is essential, a physical assignment and tuning review helps you prescribe what exactly should be upgraded.

8

Delivering the Audit

The final stage of the audit involves a number of meetings with the system administrator or the person designated to manage the shared UNIX resource. These meetings enable you to accomplish two things:

- Review all findings to date
- Include the system administrator's input, concerns, and requests in your report prior to its formal publication

In most instances, the system administrator has been an integral part of the audit and will be a key player in the future implementation of actions called for. It is essential that the system administrator take ownership of the findings and conclusions.

The Reports

Chapter 2 discusses the audit plan deliverable at length. It describes two reports: one for the chief or funding executive concerned about the business implication of the audit's findings, and the other for MIS or line managers who have both strategic and tactical responsibilities.

Both reports must be introduced based on the context of the type of audit that was conducted and what audit activities were funded. These factors make one audit different from another.

The executive report

The judgments you make based on the evidence you've found are far more valuable than the records of your measurements. Once the audit and its conclusions are prepared using the outline and definitions in chapter 2, you still need to make recommendations and comment on their costs and benefits. The recommendation part of the audit will take more or less time depending on the results of your findings, the number of departments affected, and the number of suppliers, products, and services that must be coordinated.

Remember that designing the best response to the audit findings is beyond the scope of performing the system audit. The point is to show management the extent of any problems in financial terms, with a generous margin for error. To that end, it would be wise to get conservative pricing for any products and services that you recommend. Even conditional costs should be clearly understood to include a wide cost range.

The management report

The watchword for the management report is *comprehensive*. You must cover all of the sections discussed in chapter 2 regardless of whether anything has changed or not. The findings are the measurements and results of interviews and reviews discussed in chapters 5 through 7.

The conclusions section of the management report should be a documented, reasoned response to the audit's findings. It is quite acceptable to present viable alternatives based on different criteria. However, you should make every effort to tell management which is the best alternative and why you think it is best.

Verbal reports

As with most consulting, the findings, conclusions, and recommendations should not come as a surprise at the end of the audit. Any organization has just so much capacity to absorb change, and audit report findings are no exception. Informal conversations and thumbnail status reports should be the constant dialogue between you and the audited system's management.

Different Audits

This book concentrates on first audits and routine audits because they are the most comprehensive and include most of the activities that must be carried out in shorter audits like upgrade and emergency audits. For example, both upgrade and emergency audits require the use of the UNIX commands described in chapter 3.

The remainder of this chapter deals with variations of audit circumstances other than "ideal" audits. As discussed in chapter 1, not all audits are the same. The following table from chapter 1 identifies different audit scenarios:

Audit circumstances	Technical staff help	User staff help	Outside support	No outside support
Routine	1	5	9	13
Upgrade	2	6	10	14
First	3	7	11	15
Emergency	4	8	12	16

We have used scenarios 1, 2, and 3 to illustrate qualities of the ideal audit. While all of the other scenarios either duplicate or approximate ideal audit procedures, they differ in some important ways depending on their specific circumstances and available resources.

Upgrade audits

An upgrade audit is designed to answer one question, "What will the impact be on my current production system?"

Some system owners believe that any upgrade should be applied as soon as possible in order to achieve some benefit intended by the software distributor. This notion is not well-founded. Upgrades have about a 50 percent chance of affecting a production operation. That is, not all upgrades are relevant to how an organization uses its UNIX system. Another reason for caution is to coordinate upgrades with other software products running on the system. And finally, there's the old adage, "If it's not broke, don't fix it."

Once you determine that the upgrade will be beneficial and that all other software products on the system will not be adversely affected, read the release notes and question the distributor about the following points:

1. What are the new features of this release?

2. What software corrections are included?

3. Will there be any change in the size of the system's disk storage required to use this upgrade?

4. Does the upgrade impose any restrictions not currently implemented by the installed UNIX system?

If you have technical staff help, getting someone to implement the upgrade is not a problem. Otherwise you must depend on the software supplier or a third-party consultant. In any case, you must be responsible for your system. Create a full system backup (two copies) before allowing any upgrade activities to begin.

You can use the audit software (`capture` and `compare` programs) to tightly control the upgrade. That is, you should have a specific list of software that will be added, deleted, or changed by the upgrade. Run `capture` to create a pre-upgrade baseline and run it again after the upgrade. You can then use `compare` program to accurately measure the differences caused by the upgrade.

Prior to the upgrade, follow this procedure:

1. Create a pre-upgrade baseline as follows:

```
mkdir /home/baseline/pre_update
capture / /home/baseline/pre_update PRE-UPDATE
```

2. Copy the pre-update baseline audit results to removable media.

3. Remove the baseline from the system:

```
cd /home/baseline
rm -r pre_update
```

After the upgrade, follow this procedure:

1. Create a post-upgrade baseline as follows:

```
mkdir /home/baseline/post_update
capture / /home/baseline/post_update POST-UPDATE
```

2. Copy the post-update baseline audit results to removable media.

3. Restore the pre-update directory structure.

4. Compare pre- and post-update audits as follows:

```
compare /home/baseline/pre_update /home/baseline/post _update
```

5. Print out the DIFFERENCE files to analyze the changes. The following gives you a list (printed on the default printer) of directories that have changed:

```
du -a /home/baseline/post_update | grep DIFFERENCE | pg | lp
```

Review the list and identify any directories that look suspicious.

6. Create and execute the following shell script:

```
du -a /home/baseline/post_update | grep DIFFERENCE > myfile
```

This script generates an intermediate file (`myfile`) containing the full pathnames of all of the DIFFERENCE files to be used by the shell script in step 8.

7. Use **vi** to edit out the full pathnames of DIFFERENCE files that you don't need printed out. (This step isn't necessary if you want to print all of the files.)

8. Create and execute the following shell script:

```
for files in 'cat myfile'
do
        pr $files | lp
done
```

This shell script loops through each line of the file created in the last steps (equal to the full pathname of a DIFFERENCE file) and prints its contents on your default printer.

9. Meet with the system administrator to go over the printouts of the DIFFERENCE files. There should be at least a plausible explanation if not outright documentation to explain all of the differences.

Once you've established that the upgrade was successful, the system should be made available to resume its normal services and the post-update baseline should become the latest baseline to be used in the next audit.

Emergency audit

If you've never performed a UNIX audit before, an emergency audit is not the kind to learn on. You must have UNIX experience and/or be an accomplished UNIX system administrator to perform this audit.

Chapter 1 began with a "doomsday" scenario. I'm sure you can dream up, or might even have experienced, similarly distressing experiences. In these situations, crossing all of the *t*'s and dotting all of the *i*'s is not important. The focus is on short-term survival where the objective is to buy time to stabilize the situation. If no support is available, doing a comprehensive system audit can be fatal if the production system cannot be fully restored, or if there isn't enough documentation to administer the system.

Make sure that all distribution files are available. They should be read to be certain that they can be used to restore the files systems. If they can't be read or are missing, get a readable copy before doing any major system work that involves removing or initializing any UNIX system program or data files from the disk. In the extreme case in which the manufacturer has gone out of business and you don't know of any hardware support organization supporting the system, a call for help on a popular bulletin board available from such services as CompuServe will usually bring a helpful response. Chances are good that some other person or company will know of or be using a system like yours that is currently supported. From there you should have direct access to distribution media, consulting help, and possibly third-party support for both hardware and software.

In rare instances even a basic level of support through documentation is not available. The fact is, you waited too long. Your only alternative in that case is to transfer your files onto a new system that can be supported. If you decide to do this, system integrity is not your main concern. The removal of your company records becomes the most important task.

There are two things to keep in mind here. The first is whether your records are maintained in a proprietary file structure. That is, will you need proprietary software to read the contents of your files? If the answer to that question is yes, the second thing is that you might be restricted by the proprietary software as to what computer you can move to.

You must find a compatible system to move to. If there is no compatible system to your liking, you might still need to move to someone else's compatible computer to unload your data from its proprietary structure for use with more suitable software.

Experimentation is helpful here. In recent years standardization of underlying CPU and memory technologies have made more likely the chances of running software on a different machine without having to recompile.

But let's discuss the case where your system has a viable future and a reasonable set of resources. Let's assume that the following resources are in place:

- Competent technical staff
- Original documents or exact copies of them
- Maintenance agreements for both hardware and software

Typical reasons for this case.   Frankly, it is not likely that an emergency audit would be required when so many good resources are present and available. It is more realistic to imagine an emergency caused by a project out of control or by the departure of a key developer or the suspected tampering by a disgruntled employee. However, some situations fall into the emergency category because of the lack of management foresight or planning. Suppose, for example, that the corporate auditors suddenly show up for their annual audit expecting some form of published accountability from MIS to review. In many companies, *emergency* means that employees cannot do their jobs until the system is made available to them.

Assumptions.   The basic assumption in an emergency audit is that a shared UNIX system has been withdrawn from use due to unexplainable problems that are not readily testable. The issue can be one of data integrity, corrupted software, or the unavailability of resources required by the operating system.

Discussion. Let's distinguish between being asked to find out the cause of a serious system problem, and the discovery and documentation of a systematic problem that is likely to recur. System administrators and senior system types are fairly good at tracking down immediate causes to problems. Because of their other duties, however, they often don't have the time (and in many instances, the experience) to uncover systematic causes and recommend preventative solutions.

In other words, the reason you are auditing the system is not to repair it. Rather, you must find out why the system gets into trouble and what the alternative might be for long-term, problem-free usage.

Approach. First, you need to decide on the scope of your investigation and the form of your response. If it turns out that you are asked to "do whatever it takes to get the system up," don't think you are doing an audit. You are being asked to be a troubleshooter or a problem solver. Clarify just what an audit is, and see if enough time can be provided for you to do a minimal inspection and report once the system is brought up.

Assuming that you are granted the time you need, run through the basics first, and then focus on the cause of the emergency and proceed from there.

Methodology of the Emergency Audit

In an emergency audit, the short length of time you will probably be given to audit the system will prohibit a lengthy or comprehensive investigation and report. The key here is to propose a phased response. Phase 1 should be to stabilize the system and make it useful again. Phase 2 should more closely follow the guidelines discussed in previous chapters to the extent that they need to be done.

Phase 1

Before you can begin normal audit procedures, the immediate problem must be identified and fixed. To do this, you must have the following:

1. *Stability.* If the system is inoperable, it needs to be working before any audit inspections of the computer system itself can be made. Get technical resources assigned to get the system running again. (If you are the technical resource as well as the auditor, then you must get the system operational first.) Once it's operational, do a full system backup.

2. *Interviews.* Interview the system's administrator and the technical support staff who know the most about the immediate problems and what was used to fix or work around them. Find out if the problems are cyclic or can be associated with a specific set of external events.

3. *Documentation.* Go through both the site's procedure manual and the system log to discover earlier instances of the immediate or related problems.

4. *Background.* Review any past audit reports or system status reports if they exist. Find out how much software development is being done on the system right now.

Based on what you have discovered and the remedy of the immediate problem, you are ready to begin Phase 2's system inspection. Your inspection depends on whether this is the first UNIX audit. If it is not, you'll have plenty of reliable information that was saved from the last audit. You will also have the same tools to develop similar information as well as the capability of automatically comparing the current information with the last audit.

Phase 2 If there was a previous audit

Drawing on information from previous audits, perform your inspection by following these steps:

1. Run the baseline `capture` program as follows:

```
mkdir /home/baseline/audit92
cd /home/baseline/audit92
capture / /home/baseline/audit92 audit1092
```

Save this new baseline on removable media before continuing.

2. Reload the last `capture` data set into a separate directory for comparison using this command line:

```
mkdir /home/baseline/audit91
```

Use `tar`, `cpio`, or some other utility to load the old audit results down from your removable media into the directory you just created.

3. Run `compare` to measure what has changed:

```
compare /home/baseline/audit91 /home/baseline/audit92
```

If you want to print out all of the DIFFERENCE files, use the following shell script:

```
for dname in 'cat /baseline/audit92'/DIRECTORIES''
        do
                cd $dname
                if [ -f 'DIFFERENCE' ]
                then
                        pr | lp DIFFERENCE
                fi
        done
```

4. If you want to print a portion of the DIFFERENCE files, then pull off a list of directories that have changed since the last audit. Use the following shell commands:

```
du -a /home/baseline/audit92 | grep DIFFERENCE | pg | lp
```

This gives you a list (printed on the default printer) of directories that have changed. Review the list and identify any directories that look suspicious.

5. Create and execute the following shell script:

```
du -a /home/baseline/audit92 | grep DIFFERENCE > myfile
```

This script generates an intermediate file (myfile) containing the full pathnames of all of the DIFFERENCE files to be used by the shell script in step 7.

6. Use vi to edit out the full pathnames of DIFFERENCE files that you don't need printed out.

7. Create and execute the following shell script:

```
for files in 'cat myfile'
do
    pr $files | lp
done
```

This shell script loops through each line of the file created in the last steps (equal to the full pathname of a DIFFERENCE file) and prints its contents on your default printer.

8. Meet with the system administrator to go over the printouts of the DIFFERENCE files. There should be at least a plausible explanation if not outright documentation to explain all of the differences.

Be especially sensitive to changes in the /etc directory, the addition or removal of software programs, and any unexplained usage of disk space.

Phase 2 If there was no previous audit

If there is no information available from previous audits, perform your inspection by following these steps:

1. Check the system's disk space resource to be certain there is enough space and that the space that is used is accounted for. To measure the amount of free disk space, use the following shell command:

```
df -t
```

This displays the number of free blocks versus the total blocks on all mounted file systems.

To audit how space is being used, use the following shell command:

```
du -a / > myfile
```

If you have a 132-column printer available, use the following shell command to get a formatted listing for review:

```
pr -2 -w132 myfile | lp
```

Review the listing with the system's administrator to determine if the disk usage is realistic based on how the system is being used.

2. Check the system's security. This calls for a physical inspection of how and where users have access through local and remote terminals or other attached computers. Find out who has `root` or `admin` password access. Ask for and inspect all labeled backups. Find out how frequently they are made and how they are stored.

3. Inspect the system's password file using the following shell command:

```
ls -l /etc/passwd
```

The date displayed will be the last time the password file was modified. Ask the system administrator if that date seems reasonable.

4. Check to see if all account logins have passwords using the following shell command:

```
pg /etc/passwd
```

If the password field is empty ("::") for any login account, that login account has free access to the system. In the early days of UNIX, some suppliers, anticipating they would be providing service, delivered UNIX operating system software with an open login for themselves so they could provide "manufacturer support" via remote login.

Inspection of this file will also reveal how many user accounts are supported by the system. Ask if any of these accounts are inactive. If so, they should probably be removed. Inspection will also tell you which command interpreters are being used by each login account.

If user accounting has been enabled, you should review both the user reports by login account and monthly command totals information to see just how the system is being used. If user accounting is not enabled, enabling it now will help for future audits.

5. Create a baseline for this audit by running the `capture` software as follows:

```
mkdir /home/baseline/audit92
```

```
cd /home/baseline/audit92
```

```
capture / /home/baseline/audit92 audit1092
```

Note that this will tie up the terminal from which you run it; if possible, run it overnight before you leave for the day.

6. While it is probably overkill to print out all of the README files, it would be a very good way to make an accurate and thorough review of all of the data and programs on your UNIX system. If you want to print out all of the README files in the shadow directory structure, proceed as follows:

```
du -a /home/baseline/audit92 | grep README | pg | lp
```

   This gives you a list (printed on the default printer) of each directory's audit results. Review the list and determine any directories that look suspicious. Use the following procedure to print out the README files:

```
du -a /home/baseline/audit92 | grep README > myfile
```

7. Use **vi** to edit out the full pathnames of README files that you don't need printed out. (This step isn't necessary if you want to print all of the files.)

8. Create and execute the following shell script:

```
for files in 'cat myfile'
do
    pr $files | lp
done
```

   This shell script loops through each line of the file created in the last steps (equal to the full pathname of a DIFFERENCE file) and prints its contents on your default printer.

9. Meet with the system administrator to go over the printouts of the README files. There should be at least a plausible explanation if not outright documentation to explain all of the differences.

   Now is a good time to focus on the contents of the README files and what those contents can tell you. The README file in the root directory of the audit is different than the README files in all of the shadow directories under the audit directory. It is instructive to repeat an earlier example of the README file created in the baseline's root:

```
Audit Name: FIRST  Time: Tue Sep 17 13:26:27 EDT 1991
Root Directory Examined: /
Root Directory of Baseline: /usr/audits/1991
Count of Directories in Baseline: 329
/usr/audits/1991/DIRECTORIES
UNIX Kernel File Name: dgux
```

```
UNIX Version: Pass Y (starter)
UNIX Release Number: 4.31.
System Node Name: no_node
UNIX Machine Name: Aviion
System Free Space by File System
logical: / Physical: (/dev/dsk/root 26610 blocks 5272 files
logical: /usr Physical: (/dev/dsk/usr 569 blocks 206 files
Total Blocks Used by All File Systems: 775
```

The information in this README file provides you with all of the pertinent summary information so you know what exactly has been audited, what hardware exists, what UNIX version is being used, the size of the system, what exactly was examined, and where the baseline's root directory begins.

The README files in the rest of the shadow directories are different. They provide detailed information about the directory in general (in the header portion of the README) as well as detailed information about each file in that directory (in the variable portion of the README).

The header or fixed portion of the README file tells you who owns the directory followed by how many directory files, linked files, executable files, and other files this directory contains. It also shows you the total number of characters contained in this directory. The variable portion of the README file contains details about each file such as: permissions, who the owner is, which group it belongs to, the size of the file in bytes, the date it was last written to, its name, checksum of the contents, and what type of file this is.

The README file is the result of the capture process. Its value lies in the fact that it is a comprehensive report of the contents of an audited directory structure. Once the baseline exists and is populated by the shadow directories and their README files, these READMEs themselves can be interrogated, compared, and reported on using simple shell script commands. That is, the work of getting the pertinent information about each file and directory has already been done by **capture**. Furthermore, it's been done under controlled conditions at a specific date and time.

It will be helpful to give a few examples of how you could find information about the entire UNIX system by using shell scripts to interrogate the README Files. The scripts assume that the DIRECTORIES file is still present in your baseline directory.

Let's say you needed room in a file system and you wanted to see what was involved in moving all of your **troff** and **nroff** files onto their own file system or onto another computer in the company's network. You would need more than a list of **roff** files which you could obtain by recursively invoking the **file** command for each file in the system.   Then you'd want to know who owns the directory and the file to ask or inform about your proposed reorganization. Moreover, you would probably need to see some of the other files that were present in the directories where the **roff** files were located so you could make a more informed transfer decision. In short, you'd best be served by the entire content of the README file in each directory where a **roff** file was located. The following shell script prints those README files for the audit92 directory:

```
for dname in 'cat /baseline/audit92'/DIRECTORIES''
do
    cd $dname
    if [ -f 'README' ]
    then
            grep [nt]roff README > temproff
            if [ -s 'temproff' ]
            then
                    pr | lp README
            fi
    fi
    rm temproff
done
```

10. After you and the system administrator have reviewed the README file, continue the audit by inspecting files in the **/etc** directory, following these steps:
    —Print out the contents of **/etc/fstab** using the following command:

    pg /etc/fstab

    This provides a list of all file systems that should be attached when you are at the multi-user run level. Be sure they are attached and available for inspection.
    —Print out group usage information using this command:

    pg /etc/group

    This will show you a list of all defined groups, along with who is in which group.
    —Print out the initial startup command file using this command:.

    pg /etc/inittab

    This will list all of the programs or shell scripts that are executed at each new run level. It will also tell you what the serial port assignments are for this system.

11. Check both system and user customized profiles to see if they could be a cause for concern by printing out the system profile. Use the following command:

    pr /etc/profile | lp

Review the profile to see what a new account user's (uncustomized) environment is like. This report reveals information about the default time zone, terminal type, search paths, and file creation mask (initial permission settings).

To find each user's customized profile if one exists, search all user home directories for .`profile` file. Use the following commands:

```
cd /home
du -a | grep \.profile | pg
```

This displays all of the customized user profiles at your terminal. If you prefer to print them instead, do the following:

```
cd /home
du -a | grep \.profile | pr | lp
```

Inspect user login scripts for any sort of startup or exit routines that might inhibit the system for other users. Pay special attention to `umask` and `ulimit` settings.

12. Check for installed software products as follows:

```
cd /var/opt
ls -l
```

Ask the system administrator if they are still actively used. Presumably, most of the directory entries in this directory listing represent one installed software product apiece. In older versions of UNIX, these software products are likely to be installed in the `/usr/bin` directory.

Typical Outcomes

So what do all of these procedures tell you? In general you are looking for a lack of resources and/or a lack of control. These are usually the causes of recurring, systematic problems. Your investigation might turn up other things, like errors or poor resource management. Errors and poor resource management have fairly simple solutions, while lack of resources or control take planning, implementation, and evaluation before they are remedied.

Before concluding your analysis, meet once again with the system administrator and the technical staff. Test your interpretations with their help. Discuss your ideas about what alternatives are ideally the best courses of action. Listen to their response to your alternatives. They will temper some of your ideas with a dose of reality. Heed their comments in your final report.

Costs and Benefits

The costs and benefits of adding resources and improving control vary depending on what you find. After an emergency audit, it might be an ideal time to present the real costs of deferring the installation of correctly sized resources in a timely way.

Likely Next Steps

Next steps usually involve presenting alternative responses to management. If management is convinced and decides to proceed with one of your recommendations, a project work plan is in order. It would be best if the project plan were authored by someone on the technical staff. Your role should be to advise and review the plan to ensure that it meets the audit goals you have recommended.

If the Resources Are Different

We've just finished discussing a response to an emergency audit. For this example, we were lucky enough to have in house technical staff help. But what happens if there is no technical staff? What happens if only outside technical support is available? What happens if no outside technical staff is in place or familiar with your system? If you are a consultant who audits many systems, it won't be long before you will need to deal with little or no system owner resources.

Realize that your client or sponsor know they're in serious trouble. They are looking for the proverbial "silver bullet" to magically restore what looks very lost or inaccessible.

This type of situation is very dangerous because information you are told might be completely useless. Nontechnical users will try to be helpful, and in so doing will tell you things they think happened, work, or don't work using terminology they might have heard but do not really understand. If you find yourself in this situation, listen to everything and believe nothing. Measure everything you're told, and start to distinguish between the accurate information providers and those who are trying to be helpful but are ineffective.

For example, if someone says, "The system was fully backed up each night," respond as follows:

1. Ask to see the tape(s).

2. Have them show you how they backed the system up. This tells you what the format of the backup is.

3. It's possible to do a backup using a supplier-provided shell script. First find the shell script, which should reveal the tape's format. Read the backup tape according to that format without restoring the files. If the format is either a `tar` or `cpio`, use the `-t` and `-v` options to get the table of contents you need to inspect. For example, if the backup is in

cpio format, get the contents into a file called contents, where tape is the logical name assigned to the backup tape device, using the following:

```
cpio -itv </dev/tape | tee contents
```

If the tape you are reading is one of a set of tapes, use cpio's multi-volume option -V. Your command line would be as follows:

```
cpio -itvV </dev/tape | tee contents
```

4. If the tape is readable and contains all of the files in the named backup (a count comparison will do), you can start to believe not only that the backup was executed as claimed but that the tape system works!

To obtain a count of files that were supposedly backed up, go to the root directory where the backup began and use a command that sends a recursive file listing to the standard output, then count the lines:

```
cd /backup_root
ls -r | wc -l
```

5. If you want to double-check that the backup was done as of last night, check the date and time the computer thinks it is. Then check the date and time of a file you know was written to just prior to the backup by scanning the contents file created in step 3.

These steps gives you a good idea of a thorough investigation. Do you understand the idea of supporting claims with evidence you can develop?

Proceed with Caution

Reading a backup tape that was recently created is one thing; reading a distribution tape that is two years old is another. Often, tape drive heads "creep" out of alignment. Tapes that are written and read within months of each other might be perfectly fine, while tapes that were created several months ago might no longer be within the tape head tolerances.

Another fun experience is to find out the tape was a third-party "add on" and that the driver software is nowhere to be found or is unreadable.

The point is, before doing a full audit that involves restoring the distribution, make sure that the full backup you do prior to restoring the original UNIX distribution can be read back in after the capture process is run on the distribution. You are asking for trouble if you just proceed under the assumption of how things should be.

9

Forms for the
Management Report

The management report is the organized presentation of findings and evidence that will support your conclusions and recommendations. This chapter helps you collect the "manual" portion of the evidence required to do a thorough UNIX audit by providing pre-formatted forms for gathering the information that should be included. Use these forms as checklists when creating your report.

The forms presented here are simple:

- Request for proposal audit form
- System proposal audit form
- Vendor quotation audit form
- Product receipt and warranty audit form
- Software license and support audit form
- Hardware maintenance and support audit form
- Application user interview audit form
- Technical user interview addendum
- System user interview addendum

The forms are presented in roughly the order in which they would be used. These forms put into practice the discussions in chapters 2 and 5.

All of the forms here were created using Microsoft's Excel spreadsheet program. They are included on the diskette that you can optionally send away for, using the coupon in the back of this book.

Request for Proposal Audit Form

The form in Figure 9.1 is designed to clarify the original intent of the audited system. Use it to help you evaluate how well or poorly the audited system meets its objectives.

Use one of these forms for each system you audit.

Audit Name:
Audit Date:
Auditor:
Name of System or Project:
Date RFP was published:
RFP Author(s):
Deadline For Response:
Summary of Request:
Criteria To be used For Selection:
List of Vendors RFP Sent To:
Vendors Invited To Final Discussions:

Figure 9.1 Request for proposal audit form.

Audit Name:
Audit Date:
Auditor:
Name of System or Project:
Vendor Name:
Date of Vendor Proposal:
Elaped Time of Full Implementation:
Summary of Proposal:
Favorable Aspects of Proposal:
Unfavorable Aspects of Proposal:
List of Required Adjustments:

Figure 9.2 System proposal audit form.

System Proposal Audit Form

The form in Figure 9.2 records a summary of all of the proposals received in response to the Requests for Proposal. It includes judgments and opinions of the purchasers as well as any adjustment requests that were made to the vendor.

Use one of these forms for each vendor who responds with a detailed quotation.

Vendor Quotation Audit Form

The form in Figure 9.3 gives a detailed record of what was proposed. Detailed description and cost information is collected as well as what request this item satisfies in the original RFP.

This is a two-page form. The item numbers on the second page are intentionally left out so that you can make as many copies as necessary, depending on the number of items in the system you are auditing.

Use one of these forms for each vendor who responds with a detailed quotation.

Audit Name:

Audit Date:

Auditor:

Name of System or Project:

Proposed Item			Vendor Name:			
#	Part Name	Qty	Model	Descrip.	Amount	Request Satisfied
1						
2						
3						
4						
5						
6						
7						
8						

Figure 9.3 Vendor quotation audit form.

#	Part Name	Qty	Model	Descrip.	Amount	Request Satisfied

Strike a Total of Amount after last item. --------->

Figure 9.3 *Continued.*

Product Receipt and Warranty Audit Form

The form in Figure 9.4 establishes the warranty eligibility and coverage of all system components. It reveals any basis for claims by either buyer or seller that could alter warranty eligibility.

This is a two-page form. The item numbers on the second page are intentionally left out so that you can make as many copies as necessary, depending on the number of items in the system you are auditing.

Audit Name:

Audit Date:

Auditor:

Name of System or Project:

Purchased Item			Vendor Name:							
#	Part Name	Qty	Model	Amount Quoted	Amount Charged	Date Received	Date Accepted	Date Paid	Warranty Start Date	Warranty End Date
1										
2										
3										
4										
5										
6										
7										
8										

Figure 9.4 Product receipt and warranty audit form.

#	Part Name	Qty	Model	Amount Quoted	Amount Charged	Date Received	Date Accepted	Date Paid	Warranty Start Date	Warranty End Date
Total Amount after last item. ---->										

Figure 9.4 *Continued.*

Software License and Support Audit Form

The form in Figure 9.5 is an audit of all software licenses that were purchased. Enough information is recorded to determine the support status of each software product.

This is a two-page form. The item numbers on the second page are intentionally left out so that you can make as many copies as necessary, depending on the number of items in the system you are auditing.

Audit Name:

Audit Date:

Auditor:

Name of System or Project:

Software Products

#	Product Name	Software Version No.	Vendor Name	Customer Support No.	Date Original License Received	Warranty End Date	Continuing Support Start Date	Continuing Support End Date
1								
2								
3								
4								
5								
6								
7								
8								

Figure 9.5 Software license and support audit form.

Software Products

#	Product Name	Software Version No.	Vendor Name	Customer Support No.	Date Original License Received	Warranty End Date	Continuing Support Start Date	Continuing Support End Date

Figure 9.5 *Continued.*

Hardware Maintenance and Support Audit Form

The form in Figure 9.6 records both maintenance agreement information and insurance status information on all system components. Fill out a separate form for each different maintenance organization.

This is a two-page form. The item numbers on the second page are intentionally left out so that you can make as many copies as necessary, depending on the number of items in the system you are auditing.

Audit Name:

Audit Date:

Auditor:

Name of System or Project:

Hardware Product		Maintenance Supplier				Contact Name & Tel:				
#	Product Name	Manufacturer	Warranty Begin Date	Warranty End Date	Continuing Support Start Date	Continuing Support End Date	Insurance Type	Insurance Exp. Date	Insurance Carrier	
1										
2										
3										
4										
5										
6										
7										
8										

Figure 9.6 Hardware maintenance and support audit form.

Hardware Product		Maintenance Supplier					Contact Name & Tel:				
#	Product Name	Manufacturer	Warranty Begin Date	Warranty End Date	Continuing Support Start Date	Continuing Support End Date	Insurance Type	Insurance Exp. Date	Insurance Carrier		

Figure 9.6 *Continued.*

Application User Interview Audit Form

Figure 9.7 is a fairly detailed two-page questionnaire to record information from everyone you interview who uses the system.

Audit Name:	Page 1 of 2
Audit Date:	Interviewee:
Auditor:	Department:
Usage:	
What do you use the computer for?	
How many others use the computer in the same or similar manner?	
What are the average start and stop times of each type of usage? Daily? Weekly? Monthly?	
Are there peak usage periods? If so, what are they?	
What, if any, changes have there been since the last audit?	
Security:	
Describe security habits among users.	
How frequently are passwords changes?	
Do users log out when they leave their terminals?	
Do users have remote access priveleges? How Many? If so, what are the access procedures?	
What are the security procedures in the event of employee resignation or termination?	
Do you know passwords other than your own?	
Is your pass a name, a word found in the dictionary or a numeric value easily traced to you? Is it easy to remember?	
Have there been any changes since the last audit?	
Reliability:	
How available is you system?	
How frequently has it been down?	
Does the system behave inconsistently?	
Have there been any changes since the last audit?	
Functionality:	
How does your application software work?	
What do you and don't you like about the software?	
Is the software easy to use? Does it always work the same way?	
Do "old bugs" reappear after they've been fixed?	
Have there been any changes since the last audit?	

Figure 9.7 Application user interview audit form.

Audit Name:	Page 2 of 2
Audit Date:	Interviewee:
Auditor:	Department:

Integrity:	
Does your input always "take"?	
Do you get excessive "Lock" messages?	
Have you ever had to re-enter your work?	
What, if any, changes have there been since the last audit?	

Performance:	
How responsive are your interactive sessions?	
Are some times better than others?	
Do long reports slow down interactive response time?	
Have there been any changes since the last audit?	

Service:	
What is the procedure that you follow to report problems? Request Services or enhancements?	
Are your requests acknowledged? Are they serviced in a timely manner? Explain.	

Ideal System:	
Can you describe the ideal system to work on?	
Can you quantify the effect of these features or describe the impact they would have on your work?	

Figure 9.7 *Continued.*

Technical User Interview Addendum

Figure 9.8 is an addendum to the application user interview audit form. Add these questions when you interview technical users like programmers and analysts.

Audit Name:	Page 1 of 1
Audit Date:	Interviewee:
Auditor:	Department:
Tools	
How do you develop or maintain software?	
What compilers or UNIX Utilities are you using?	
Which, if any, 3rd party development products are you using?	
How are new updates and releases of tools re-installed? How do you maintain product version compatibilities?	
What, if any, changes have there been since the last audit?	
Reliability:	
Do you know if any of the products you use are flawed? Have manufacturers or products user groups provided you with "problem" or "bug " lists?	
Have you identified the problems you need to build "workarounds" for?	
Is there are backlog of reported problems for software you have developed?	
Do you have any tracking system or records management facility to report the status and progress of reported problems?	
Have there been any changes since the last audit?	

Figure 9.8 Technical user interview addendum.

System User Interview Addendum

Figure 9.9 is an addendum to the application user interview audit form. Add these questions when you interview system users like system administrators or database administrators.

Audit Name:	Page 1 of 1
Audit Date:	Interviewee:
Auditor:	Department:
History	
What stage of system life cycle is your system in?	
What do you need and why?	
Can you discuss the evolution of the system since the last audit or since installation?	
What, if any, resources changes are being considered, proposed, or scheduled?	
Day to Day Operations:	
Discuss your regular procedures: Automated, Manual.	
What are your event driven procedures?	
Who fulfills your responsibility when you are absent or not available?	
How do you or what do you use to manage records of system events and service requests.	
Have there been any changes since the last audit?	
Support	
Rate the support you provide. Hardware? Software?	
Rate your in house software development and/or maintenance team.	
Have there been any changes since the last audit?	

Figure 9.9 System user interview addendum.

Program Listings

```
# Bourne Shell Conventions
# Author:  Michael G. Grottola
# Copyright 1992 Business Resources, Inc.
#
# Usage: capture ex_directory re_directory
#
#      Where: ex_directory is root of hierarchy to examine
#             re_directory is root of baseline repository
#         audit_name is unique baseline name
#
### TEST CAPTURE PROGRAM'S INVOCATION FOR ITS VALIDITY ###
if [ "$#" -ne 3 ]
then
      echo "Insufficient Command Arguments"
      echo " Usage: capture ex_directory re_directory"
      echo " Where: ex_directory is root of hierarchy to examine"
      echo "        re_directory is root of baseline repository"
      echo "        audit_name is unique baseline name"
      exit 1
fi

if [ ! -d $1 ]
then
      echo "Examination Root Directory does not exit. Try again."
      echo " Usage: capture ex_directory re_directory"
      echo " Where: ex_directory is root of hierarchy to examine"
      echo "        re_directory is root of baseline repository"
      echo "        audit_name is unique baseline name"
```

```
      exit 1
fi


### SET UP AND DEFINE VARIABLES USED IN THIS SHELL PROGRAM ###
ex=$1                      # Root of Directory Structure to be examined
re=$2                      # Root of Baseline Directory
auditname=$3               # Name of Audit
auditdate='date'           # Time stamp for baseline creation
dp=0                       # Count of Directories Processed
fp=0                       # Count of Files Processed
base=$re'/README'          # File containing global system or audit
                           # information
log=$re'/LOG'              # Log file for the baseline creation process
header=$re'/read.tmp'      # Temporary Header Work File (Lines 1-10 in
                           # README)
trailer=$re'/hold'         # Temporary Trailer Work File (Lines 11-"n"
                           # in README)


##CREATE A FILE, "DIRECTORIES", A LIST OF ALL DIRS TO BE EXAMINED##

clear
if [ -d $re ]
then                       # Specified baseline directory exists.
    echo "Baseline Directory Already Exists. Shall I overwrite it?"
    echo "Answer: Y or N"
    read answer
    case $answer
        in
            "Y")  echo "Clearing Directory";;
            "y")  echo "Clearing Directory";;
            "N")  echo "Returning Control to You.";exit;;
            "n")  echo "Returning Control to You.";exit;;
              *)  echo "Returning Control to You.";exit;;
        esac
    rm -r $re
fi

mkdir $re # Create baseline root first

echo "Creating list of all directories to be examined. Standby."
echo 'date'' Begin Listing Directories to be examined.' >> $log

ls -pR $ex ¦ grep : > $re/temp  #Select Directories ONLY

for list in 'cat $re/temp'          #Strip off trailing colon.
do
    length1='echo $list ¦ wc -c¦awk '{print $1}''
    length2='expr $length1 — 2'
```

```
           echo 'echo $list ¦ cut -c1-$length2' > $re/DIRECTORIES
done
rm $re/temp
echo 'date'' End Listing Directories to be examined.' >> $log
### CREATE MASTER README IN BASELINE ROOT ###

echo 'Audit Name: '$auditname'   Time: '$auditdate > $base
echo 'Root Directory Examined: '$ex >> $base
echo 'Root Directory of Baseline: '$re >> $base
echo 'date'' Begin Count of Directories in Base Line: ' >> $log
echo 'Count of Directories in Baseline: ''wc -l $re'/DIRECTORIES''\
>> $base
echo 'date'' End Count of Directories in Base Line: ' >> $log
echo 'Unix Kernel File Name: ''uname' >> $base
echo 'Unix Version: ''uname -v' >> $base
echo 'Unix Release Number: ''uname -r' >> $base
echo 'System Node Name: ''uname -n' >> $base
echo 'Unix Machine Name: ''uname -m' >> $base
echo "System Free Space by File System" >> $base
echo 'df¦sed -n 1,1p¦awk '{print "logical: "$1" Physical:\
"$2"   "$4,$5,$6,$7}'' >> $base
echo 'df¦sed -n 2,2p¦awk '{print "logical: "$1" Physical:\
"$2"   "$4,$5,$6,$7}'' >> $base
echo 'Total Blocks Used by All File Systems: ''du -s / ¦ awk'\
{print $1}'' >> $base

### CREATE SHADOW DIRECTORY STRUCTURE ###

echo 'date'' Creating Shadow Directories.'
echo 'date'' Creating Shadow Directories: ' >> $log


[ "'echo $ex'" != "\/" ] # Special Treatment examining from root
if [ "$?" -ne 0 ]
then
     mkdir $re$ex              # Create baseline root first
else
     echo $re > /dev/null
fi
cp /home/baseline/TLIST $re   # Copy file type list to baseline
                             # for files in 'cat $re'/DIRECTO-
RIES''
do
     mkdir $re$files
done
echo 'date'' End of Shadow Directory Creation: ' >> $log
### BUILD README FILES FOR EACH DIRECTORY IN SHADOW STRUCTURE ###

echo 'date'' Begin Directory Examinations.'
echo 'date'' Begin Directory Examinations' >> $log
```

```
#  The data gathering that follows creates a README file in the
#  shadow
#  directory that consists of a fixed header part and a variable
#  trailer.
#  The fixed header part describes summary information about the
#  directory being examined. The variable trailer includes 1 line
#  for each file in the directory. The specific data captured in
#  the README file is as follows:
#
#  FIXED HEADER:
#
#  LINE #  DATA                 DESCRIPTION
#
------  -----------  --------------------------------------------
#  Line  1: Audit Name - entered interactively by auditor.

#  Line  1: Audit Time - the time and date when this program was
#  first invoked.
#  Line  2: Directory Name - Full directory name this README
#  describes.
#  Line  3: Directory Owner - Owner of examined directory.
#  Line  4: Directories - Number of Directory files in examined
#  directory.
#  Line  5: Links - Number of Linked files in examined directory.
#  Line  6: Executables - Number of Executable files in examined
#  directory.
#  Line  7: Others - Number of other types of files in examined
#  directory.
#  Line  8: Characters - Total characters in all files in examined
#  directory.
#  Line  9: Reserved - Not currently used.  Reserve for future use.
#  Line 10: Reserved - Not currently used.  Reserve for future use.
#
#  VARIABLE TRAILER:
#
#  LINE #  DATA                 DESCRIPTION
#
------  -----------  --------------------------------------------
#  Line 11: File Details - 10 detail variables per each file in
#  the directory.
#       Field  1: Permissions - Access permission code string
#       Field  2: Owner - account that owns this file
#  Field  3: Group - group that owns this file
#  Field  4: Characters - Length of this file in characters.
#  Field  5: Month - Month the file was created or last modified.
#       Field  6: Day - Day file created or modified.
#       Field  7: Time - Time/Year(if not current Yr) file created
#       or modified.
#       Field  8: Filename - Name of this file entry.
#       Field  9: Checksum - 16 bit checksum of files contents.
```

```
#       Field 10:  Type - Estimate of purpose of file based on
#       contents.

echo "Begin README Process"
tcount='wc -l $re'/'TLIST ¦ awk '{print $1}'' #Initialize the
                                              # number of types
for dname in 'cat $re'/DIRECTORIES''
do                                    #  All directories loop
    echo 'date'' Directory Name: '$dname >> $log
    dp='expr $dp + 1'
    Increment Total Directory Count
    cd $dname
    ds=0 # Directories within directory counter
    es=0 # Executables within directory counter
    ls=0 # Linked Files within directory counter
    os=0 # All Other Files within directory counter
    cs=0 # Total Characters within directory counter

    for name in 'ls'
    do  #  All Files within a single directory
        fp='expr $fp + 1'     # Increment Total File Count
        [ -z "$name" ] ; if [ $? -eq 0 ]# Do nothing if directory
                                        # is empty
        then
           break
        fi

        if [ -d $name ] # Don't report directories within
                        # directories
        then
            ds='expr $ds + 1'  # Increment Directory Header
            Counter
            continue
        fi

        if [ 'ls -l $name ¦ wc -w ¦ awk '{print $1}'' -eq 9 ]
        then
            ls -l $name ¦ awk '{print\
            ($1,$3,$4,$5,$6,$7,$8,$9)}' > $re'/'temp1
        else
            # This handles /dev node numbers
            ls -l $name ¦ awk '{print ($1,$3,$4,$5,$7,$8,$9)}'>\
            $re'/'temp1
            ls $name >> $re'/'temp1
        fi
        [ "'echo $dname'" != ."\/dev" ] # Special Treatment for\
                                        # dev directory

            if [ "$?" -ne 0 ]
            then
```

```
      echo 'sum $name' ¦ awk '{print $1}' >> $re'/'temp1
else
      echo "0" >> $re'/'temp1
fi
count=$tcount    # Set count to total number of types in
                 # "TLIST"
until [ $count -eq 0 ]  # Test all known types against
                        # "file output".
do                      # Begining of File Type Loop

    # Read in defined types from type list, "TLIST".
    #-------------------------------------------------

    sed -n $count','$count'p' $re'/'TLIST >$re'/'temp
                      #Step thru type list
    read type kind < $re'/'temp

    # Test each one until a match is found.
    #--------------------------------------

    tresult='file $name ¦ grep -i $type ¦ wc -c'
                      #Set up test
    count='expr $count - 1'

    if [ $tresult -ne 0 ]               # If match
                                        # then > 0
    then

        echo $kind >> $re'/'temp1       # Save Audit
                                        # Defined
                                        # "Kind"
        case $type                      # Update Header
                             # Counters
        in
            "executable")   es='expr $es + 1';;
             "symbolic")    ls='expr $ls + 1';;
                    *)      os='expr $os + 1';;
        esac


        [ "'echo $dname'" != "\/dev" ] # Special
                                       # Treatment for
                                       # /dev directory
        if [ "$?" -ne 0 ]
        then
            chars='wc -c $name ¦ awk '{print $1}''
        else
            chars=0
        fi
```

```
                    cs='expr $cs + $chars'
                    break    # "Kind" is unique, break loop.
                fi

            done                    # End of File Type Loop

    # If no match after full type table comparison,type is Unknown.
    #─────────────────────────────────────────────────────────────
    if [ $tresult -eq 0 ]               # If match then > 0
    then
            echo "Unknown" >> $re'/'temp1  #  Save Audit Defined "Kind"
    fi

    # Remove all newlines from temp1 and append it to "hold"
    #──────────────────────────────────────────────────────────
    tr "\012" "\040" < $re'/'temp1 > $re'/'temp2
    echo  >> $re'/'temp2
    cat $re'/'temp2 >> $trailer
done            # End of Directory Loop
# BUILD HEADER

echo $auditname' '$auditdate > $header
echo $dname >> $header
echo 'ls -al $dname ¦ sed -n 2,2p ¦ awk '{print $3}''>> $header
echo $ds >> $header
echo $ls >> $header
echo $es >> $header
echo $os >> $header
echo $cs >> $header
echo >> $header
echo >> $header

        # COMBINE HEADER AND TRAILER

        if [ -f $trailer ]
        then
            cat $trailer >> $header
            rm $trailer
        fi
        # PLACE COMBINED README INTO SHADOW DIRECTORY
        echo 'WRITING README FOR: '$dname' TO '$re$dname
        cat $header > $re'/'$dname'/README'
        rm $header
done

echo
if [ -f $re'/'temp1 ]
    then
        rm $re'/'temp*
```

```
     fi
echo 'Total Directories Processed: '$dp'   Total Files Processed:\
'$fp
echo 'Total Directories Processed: '$dp'   Total Files Processed:\
'$fp >> $log
echo 'date'' End of Directory Examinations.' >> $log
echo
echo 'date'' Baseline Processing Completed.'

# Bourne Shell Conventions
# Author:  Michael G. Grottola
# Copyright 1992 Business Resources, Inc.
#
# Usage: compare new_directory old_directory
#
#        Where: new_directory is root of the new audit to examine
#               old_directory is root of old baseline repository
#
#
##########################################################
new=$1                  # Root of Directory Structure to be
                        # examined
old=$2                  # Root of Baseline Directory
base=$old'/README'      # File containing global system or audit
                        # information
log=$old'/LOG'          # Log file for the baseline creation process

for dname in 'cat $new'/DIRECTORIES''
do                                      # All directories loop

    [ -f $old'/dname' ]
    if [ "$?" -ne 0 ]
    then
         echo $new'/dname' >> NEWDIRS
         break

    fi
    clear
    result='cmp $old'/dname' $new/dname''
    [ -z "$result" ]
    if [ "$?" = 0 ]
    then
         echo "Equal"
         exit
    else
         sed -n '1,2p' $1 > $new'/DIFFERENCE'
         for lines in 3 4 5 6 7 8
         do
                 sed -n $lines,$lines'p' $1 >>temp1
```

```
            sed -n $lines,$lines'p' $2 >>temp2
      done
      paste temp1 temp2  >> $new'/DIFFERENCE'
      echo >> $new'/DIFFERENCE'
      echo >> $new'/DIFFERENCE'
      echo  "Files That Have Changed:" >> $new'/DIFFERENCE'
      echo  "-----------------------" >> $new'/DIFFERENCE'
fi

sed -n '11,$p' $1 > temp1
sed -n '11,$p' $2 > temp2

result='cmp temp1 temp2'
[ -z "$result" ]
if [ "$?" = 0 ]
then
      echo "Equal"
      exit
else
      count1='wc -l temp1¦awk '{print $1}''
      count1='expr $count1 + 1'
      f1count=1
      count2='wc -l temp2¦awk '{print $1}''
      count2='expr $count2 + 1'
      until [ "$f1count" = "$count1" ]
      do
            sed -n "$f1count"','"$f1count"'p' temp1> line1
            name1='awk '{print $8}' line1'
            f2count=1
            until [ "$f2count" = "$count2" ]
            do
                  sed -n "$f2count"','"$f2count"'p' temp2> line2
                  name2='awk '{print $8}' line2'
                  if [ "$name1" = "$name2" ]
                  then
                      result='cmp line1 line2'
                      [ -z "$result" ]
                      if [ "$?" = 0 ]
                      then
                            break
                      else
                            cat line1 >> DIFFERENCE
                            cat line2 >> DIFFERENCE
                            break
                      fi
                  else
                        countx='expr $count2 - 1'
                        if [ $countx -eq $f2count ]
                        then
                            cat line1 >> DELETED
```

```
                         fi
                         f2count='expr $f2count + 1 '
                 fi
         done
         f1count='expr $f1count + 1 '
         done
     fi


     #### What's Been Added? ####



     f2count=1
     until [ "$f2count" = "$count2" ]
     do
         sed -N "$f2count"','"$f2count"'p' temp2> line2
         name2='awk '{print $8}' line2'
         f1count=1
         until [ "$f1count" = "$count1" ]
         do
             sed -n "$f1count"','"$f1count"'p' temp1> line1
             name1='awk '{print $8}' line1'
             if [ "$name2" = "$name1" ]
             then
                     break
             else
                     countx='expr $count1 - 1'
                     if [ $countx -eq $f1count ]
                     then
                         cat line2 >> ADDED
                     break
                     fi
                 fi
             f1count='expr $f1count + 1 '
         done
         f2count='expr $f2count + 1 '
     done
     echo >> DIFFERENCE
     echo  "Files That Have Been Deleted Since The Last\
Audit:" >> DIFFERENCE
         echo"--------------------------------------------------"\
>> DIFFERENCE
         [ -f DELETED ]
         if [ "$?" -eq 0 ]
         then
             cat DELETED >> DIFFERENCE
             rm DELETED

         else
```

```
                echo "None" >> DIFFERENCE
          fi
          echo >> DIFFERENCE
          echo  "Files That Have Been Added Since The Last\
Audit:" >> DIFFERENCE
          echo"------------------------------------------------"\
>> DIFFERENCE
          [ -f ADDED ]
          if [ "$?" -eq 0 ]
          then
                cat ADDED >> DIFFERENCE
                rm ADDED
          else
                echo "None" >> DIFFERENCE
          fi
          rm temp1 temp2 line1 line2
done


# Bourne Shell Conventions
# Author:  Michael G. Grottola
# Copyright 1992 Business Resources, Inc.
#
# Usage: diff.p DIFFERENCE
#
#     Where: DIFFERENCE is any "DIFFERENCE" file formatted by
#     "compare"
#
#
#
############################################################

sed -n '1,1p' DIFFERENCE ¦ awk '{print "Previous Audit Name: "$1"\
Audit Date:"$2,$3,$4,$5,$6,$7}'
echo "===================================================="
echo " Previous Audit Findings  Current Audit Findings  "
echo " ---------------------    ---------------------   "
sed -n '2,2p' DIFFERENCE ¦ awk ' {print "       Directory Name:\
"$1}'
sed -n '3,3p' DIFFERENCE ¦ awk '{print    " Directory Owner: "$1"\
"$2}'
sed -n '4,4p' DIFFERENCE ¦ awk '{print    " Directory Files: "$1"\
"$2}'
sed -n '5,5p' DIFFERENCE ¦ awk '{print    "    Linked Files: "$1"\
"$2}'
sed -n '6,6p' DIFFERENCE ¦ awk '{print    "Executable Files: "$1"\
"$2}'
sed -n '7,7p' DIFFERENCE ¦ awk '{print    "     Other Files: "$1"\
"$2}'
```

```
sed -n '8,8p' DIFFERENCE ¦ awk '{print   "Total Characters: "$1"\
"$2}'
echo
echo
echo "File Details: Permissions, Owner, Group, Size, Date,Name,\
Checksum, Type"
echo "--------------------------------------------------"
sed -n '11,$p' DIFFERENCE
```

B

TLIST Contents

Contents of TLIST

executable Executable
Terminfo Terminfo
English English
archive Archive
[nt]roff [nt]roff
ascii Ascii
block Block
program Program
cannot Cannot_Open
character Character
commands Commands
data Data
directory Directory
empty Empty
fifo Fifo
packed Packed
symbolic Link

Reports Generated
By Shell Programs

This report can be generated by changing directories to the audit baseline's
root and typing:

```
lp README

Audit Name: FIRST   Time: Tue Sep 17 13:26:27 EDT 1991
Root Directory Examined: /
Root Directory of Baseline: /home/baseline/fullsys
Count of Directories in Baseline:  329
/home/baseline/fullsys/DIRECTORIES
Unix Kernel File Name: dgux
Unix Version: Pass Y (starter)
Unix Release Number: 4.31.
System Node Name: no_node
Unix Machine Name: AViiON
System Free Space by File System
logical: / Physical: (/dev/dsk/root 26610 blocks 5272 files
logical: /usr Physical: (/dev/dsk/usr 56953 blocks 20696 files
Total Blocks Used by All File Systems: 109199
```

This report can be generated by changing directories to the shadow directory of interest and typing:

```
lp README

    Audit Name: FIRST          Audit Date: Mon Sep 16 15:26:11
```

```
EDT 1991
  Directory Name: /etc/erm
 Directory Owner: root
 Directory Files: 0
    Linked Files: 0
Executable Files: 2
     Other Files: 3
Total Characters: 31561


File Details: Permissions, Owner, Group, Size, Date, Name, Chksum, Type
----------------------------------------------------------------------
-rw-r—r— root sys 7454 Apr 18 1990 ermes 9660 Executable
-rw-r—r— root sys 4507 Apr 18 1990 ermes.c 61716 Ascii
-rw-r—r— root sys 8802 Apr 18 1990 extended_ermes 14152 Executable
-rw-r—r— root sys 10265 Apr 18 1990 extended_ermes.c 57937 Ascii
-rw-r—r— root sys 533 Apr 18 1990 makefile 42789 Ascii
```

This report can be generated by changing directories to the shadow directory of interest and typing:

```
diff.p DIFFERENCE ¦ lp

FIRST Mon Sep 16 15:26:11 EDT 1991
/etc/erm
root      root
0         0
0         0
2         2
3         3
31561     31571


Files That Have Changed:
----------------------------------------------------------------
-rw-r—r— root sys 4507 Apr 18 1990 ermes.c 61716 Ascii
-rw-r—r— root sys 4517 Sep 11 1990 ermes.c 25341 Ascii

Files That Have Been Deleted Since The Last Audit:
----------------------------------------------------------------
None

Files That Have Been Added Since The Last Audit:
----------------------------------------------------------------
None
```

D

Example of Sizing Template

This appendix shows an example of a template used to estimate the size of a data set based on *known external business relationships*. The template uses predefined spreadsheet relationships in order to project the number of expected records and therefore the expected size of a given business set. That is, the number of records refers to calculations based on the defined relationships.

Estimated data definition Data entity assumptions	Bytes Stats	Records	X	MB
Total number of subscribers	400,000			
Subscriber services per subscriber	1.00			
Number of distribution channels	6.00			
Number of channel members	15,000			
Number of active channel members	2,000			
Avg. no. of zip code areas served /channel member	10.00			
Avg. number of video cipher units per customer	1.10			
Total number of service package offerings	100			
Unique services (components of packages)	27.00			
Promotions per year	30.00			
Policies	20.00			
Policy rules	200			
Contracts per service package per channel member	1.00			
Orders transactions per service package	8.00			
Customer service inquiries per service package life	2.00			
Average service package life (in years)	1.00			
Consumers who receive bills	269,000			
Consumer subscriptions billed annually	188,300			
Consumer subscriptions billed monthly	80,700			
Business bills	4,000			

Estimate of total "flat" data in bytes   **6,170 MB**

Estimated data definition	Bytes	Records	X	MB	
Subscriber	**259**	**400,000**	**1**	**103.6**	**1.68%**
Subscriber number	10				
Last name	25				
First name	10				
Service address	50				
Service city	25				
Service state	2				
Service zip	10				
Bill to address	50				
Bill to city	25				
Bill to state	2				
Bill to zip	10				
Home phone	20				
Business phone	20				
Subscriber services	**115**	**400,000**	**1**	**46.0**	**0.75%**
Subscriber	10				
Service package	10				
Product assembly	10				
Channel	10				
Promotion	10				
Order ID	10				
Bill to indicator (subscriber, channel)	5				
Order date	8				
Bill date	8				
Connect date	8				
Expiration date	8				
Disconnect date	8				
Subscription type (monthly, annual)	5				
Channel method (wholesale, retail)	5				
Subscriber demo/Psycho graphics	**61**	**4,000,000**	**1**	**244.0**	**3.95%**
Subscriber	10				
Demo/Interest code	3				
Response	1				
Priority	4				
Quantity	8				
Action code	3				
Critical dates	32				
Channel	**582**	**6**	**1**	**0.0**	**0.00%**
Code	10				
Description	60				
Rule driving information	512				
Channel member	**250**	**15,000**	**1**	**3.8**	**0.06%**
Channel ID	10				
Channel name	10				
Geographic region	10				
Subscriber	10				
Address	50				
City	25				
State	2				
Zip	10				

Estimated data definition	Bytes	Records	X	MB	
Channel type	5				
Contact name	30				
Contact title	30				
Credit account number	15				
Credit account type	5				
Credit expiration date	8				
Credit limit	15				
Credit available	5				
Geographic region	**20**	**15,000**	**10**	**3.0**	**0.05%**
Channel member	10				
Zip code	10				
Product assembly	**20**	**440,000**	**1**	**8.8**	**0.14%**
Assembly number	10				
Subscriber service	10				
Assembly transactions	**31**	**880,000**	**1**	**27.3**	**0.44%**
Assembly number	10				
Transaction code	3				
Transaction date	8				
Subscriber number	10				
Service package	**65**	**100**	**1**	**0.0**	**0.00%**
Package name	20				
Package period	10				
Service	10				
Subscriber services	10				
Price	15				
Service	**60**	**27**	**1**	**0.0**	**0.00%**
Service	10				
Service package	10				
Programmer	10				
License fee rate	15				
Royalty rate	15				
Promotion	**81**	**30**	**1**	**0.0**	**0.00%**
Campaign	10				
Service package	10				
Campaign type	10				
Start date	8				
End date	8				
Channel method	5				
Subscription type	5				
Subscription length	10				
Promotion price	15				
Policy	**25**	**20**	**1**	**0.0**	**0.00%**
Subject	25				
Policy rule	**70**	**200**	**1**	**0.0**	**0.00%**
Policy	10				
Rule parameter	20				
Parameter value	20				
Parameter comparison	20				

Estimated data definition	Bytes	Records	X	MB	
Contract info	**76**	**150,000**	**1**	**11.4**	**0.18%**
Channel	10				
Contract ID	10				
Service package	10				
Contract price	15				
Contract length	10				
Contract date	8				
Contract expiration	8				
Channel method	5				
Order	**202**	**3,200,000**	**1**	**646.4**	**10.48%**
Subscriber	10				
Order ID	10				
Channel	10				
Order type	5				
Videocipher	10				
Service package	10				
Price	15				
Campaign code	10				
Order date	8				
Related to order	10				
Bill to code	10				
Bill date	8				
Payment type	5				
Credit card type	5				
Credit card no.	10				
Credit expiration date	8				
Credit authorization number	10				
Channel method	5				
Subscription type	5				
Connect date	8				
Connect acknowledgment	25				
Order status (pending, billable)	5				
Customer service inquiry	**91**	**800,000**	**1**	**72.8**	**1.18%**
Inquiry ID	10				
Channel ID	10				
Subscriber ID	10				
Inquiry type	5				
Inquiry date	8				
Inquiry status	5				
Resolution	25				
Resolved date	8				
Memo	10				
Consumer (direct) billing	**203**	**1,156,700**	**1**	**234.8**	**3.81%**
Subscriber	10				
Bill date	8				
Invoice number	10				
Subscriber service (restricted by channel method)	160				
Bill amount	15				

Estimated data definition	Bytes	Records	X	MB	
Business billing	203	4,000	1	0.8	0.01%
Channel	10				
Bill date	8				
Invoice number	10				
Subscriber service (grouped by					
channel method)	160				
Bill amount					
	15				
Consumer payment	48	1,156,700	1	55.5	0.90%
Subscriber	10				
Payment ID	10				
Payment date	8				
Payment amount	15				
Payment type					
	5				
Business payment	48	4,000	1	0.2	0.00%
Channel	10				
Payment ID	10				
Payment date	8				
Payment amount	15				
Payment type	5				
Commission program	10	15,000	1	0.2	0.00%
Commission program	10				
Commission rule	195	15,000	1	2.9	0.05%
Commission program	10				
Subscriber service (restricted by					
subs. service fields & values)	160				
Channel (restricted by channel method)	10				
Commision rate	15				
Renewal campaign	165	21,833	1	3.6	0.06%
Subscriber	10				
Expiration date	8				
Renew status	3				
Next action	3				
Last handled by	10				
Last action	3				
Renew information (who, when, etc.)	128				
Reseller applications	138	300	1	0.0	0.00%
Channel member	10				
Application information	128				
Reseller commission transactions	34	2,000	12	0.8	0.01%
Channel member	10				
Transaction type	3				
Transaction date	8				
Transaction amount	10				
Transaction code	3				

Programmer commission transactions	**34**		**30**	**12**	**0.0**	**0.00%**
Programmer	10				
Transaction type					
	3				
Estimated data definition	**Bytes**	**Records**	**X**	**MB**	
Transaction date	8				
Transaction amount	10				
Transaction code	3				
Invoice image	**4,000**	**1,160,700**	**1**	**4642.8**	**75.25%**
Image of invoice for reference & reprint	4,000				
Test model	**0**		**1**	**1**	**61.1**	**0.99%**
1 percent of total database					

E

Audit-type
Decision Flowchart

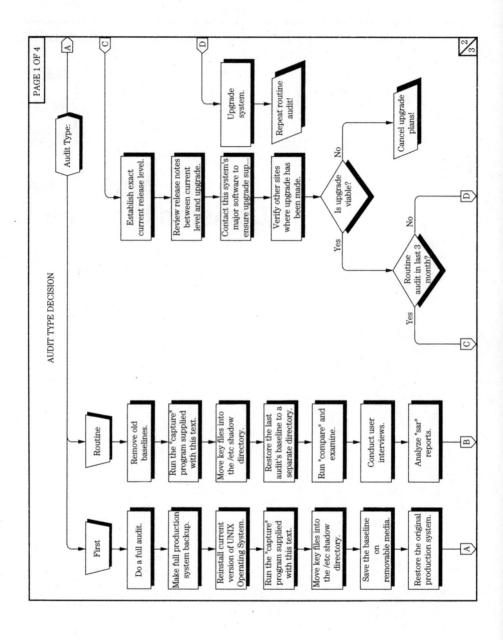

AUDIT TYPE DECISION

PAGE 1 OF 4

Audit Type:

First

- Do a full audit.
- Make full production system backup.
- Reinstall current version of UNIX Operating System.
- Run the "capture" program supplied with this text.
- Move key files into the /etc shadow directory.
- Save the baseline on removable media.
- Restore the original production system.

A

Routine

- Remove old baselines.
- Run the "capture" program supplied with this text.
- Move key files into the /etc shadow directory.
- Restore the last audit's baseline to a separate directory.
- Run "compare" and examine.
- Conduct user interviews.
- Analyze "sar" reports.

B

- Establish exact current release level.
- Review release notes between current level and upgrade.
- Contact this system's major software to ensure upgrade sup...
- Verify other sites where upgrade has been made.

Is upgrade viable?

No → Cancel upgrade plans!

Yes → Routine audit in last 3 month?

No → D

Yes → C

- Upgrade system.
- Repeat routine audit!

C

D

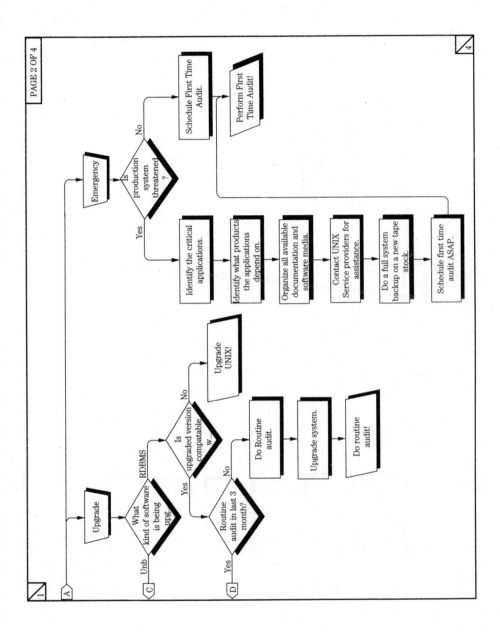

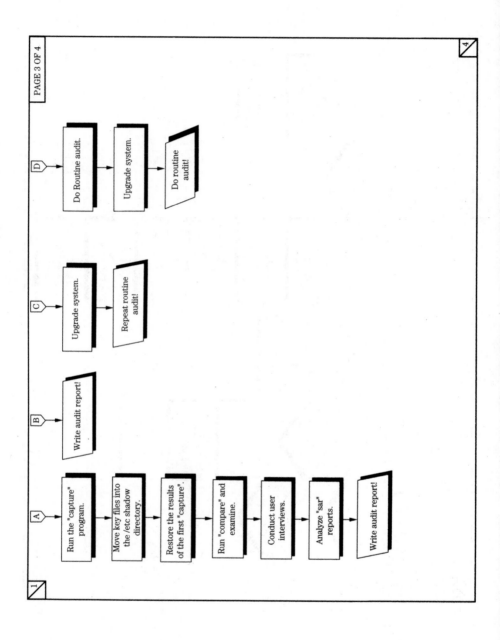

Index

ABOUT THE AUTHOR

Michael G. Grottola has designed systems, developed software, and audited systems for over twenty years. A software engineering authority, Mr. Grottola is the author of a series of articles about the software development lifecycle, UNIX and OS/2, and various topics in communications. He is currently the president of Business Resources, a software engineering consulting firm in New Jersey.

The UNIX Audit

If you are intrigued with the possibilities of the programs and forms offered in the *The UNIX Audit*, you might want to order the companion source code disk containing the latest versions of the programs, data files, and forms found in the Appendices and Chapter 9 of the text. This diskette will save you hours of typing and eliminate the possibility of introducing human errors.

The files described above are available on either 5¼" or 3½" diskettes for $24.95 plus $2.50 per disk for shipping and handling. The program and data files will be sent to you in ASCII format. The forms will be sent to you in spread-sheet format (XLS Version 4.0 or later). Your diskettes will be shipped via first-class mail within two weeks of your prepaid order.

Yes, I'm interested. Please send me the latest versions of the programs, files, and forms contained in *The UNIX Audit*.

    ____   copies 5¼" disk, $24.95 each . . . . . . $ _____

    ____   copies 3½" disk, $24.95 each . . . . . . $ _____

Shipping & Handling: $2.50 per disk in U.S.
                 ($5.00 per disk outside the U.S.) $ _____

❏ Check here if you have included suggestions for changes or enhancements to the UNIX Tools published in *The UNIX Audit*.

❏ Check or money order enclosed made payable to Business Resources, Inc.

Your shipping address (Please print or type clearly):

Name _____

Address _____

City_____ State_____ Zip _____

Send this order to:

Business Resources, Inc.
473 East Saddle River Road
Upper Saddle River, New Jersey 07458-1774